THE BOOK OF
DINOSAURS

THE NATURAL HISTORY MUSEUM GUIDE

THE BOOK OF
DINOSAURS

THE NATURAL HISTORY MUSEUM GUIDE

TIM GARDOM
with
ANGELA MILNER
Scientific Adviser

Prima Publishing
P.O. Box 1260 G&M
Rocklin, CA 95677
(916) 786-0426

PRIMA

THIS IS A CARLTON BOOK

For Christine Hayek, Samuel, Peter and Keziah

Originally published as The Natural History Museum Book of Dinosaurs
Copyright © 1993 The Natural History Museum, London
Design copyright © 1993 Carlton Books Limited

Prima Publishing, Rocklin, CA 95677

Printed and bound in Italy

96 95 94 93 10 9 8 7 6 5 4 3 2 1

ISBN 1-55958-350-9

CONTENTS

FOREWORD

There are few groups of animals, living or extinct, that pique the human imagination like the dinosaurs. Although dinosaurs have been extinct for 65 million years, a majority of people are able not only to recognize their skeletons, but also to remember many of their different scientific names. We humans are more familiar with the scientific names and skeletons of dinosaurs than we are with any group of living animals, including the mammals of which we are a member. Whether it be the dinosaurs' great success or ultimate failure, their size or simply that they were peculiar, in the eyes of most humans dinosaurs are the superstars of evolution. Animals so successful that their extinction worries even us.

As discoveries of more dinosaur remains are made throughout the world our ideas and views of these extinct creatures are evolving. We are coming closer to unraveling the mysteries of their ancient lives and the environments in which they lived. In the past, with few skeletons, an abundance of preconceived notions and little data, the dinosaur world was viewed very differently than it is now. Dinosaurs were thought of as gigantic, stupid, cold-blooded freaks of nature, that roamed the Earth searching for a place in time to go extinct. But new collecting efforts, with detailed studies of their skeletons, behavior and ecology, have resulted in a fresh, new picture of these incredible animals, a picture that reveals them as equally adapted to their place in time as we are to ours.

The Book of Dinosaurs is a book for all ages that takes the reader on a journey through the present facts and past fictions of our historical understanding of these extinct animals, and the world in which they lived. It is a book based on our current thoughts, ideas and discoveries as portrayed in The Natural History Museum's new and exciting dinosaur exhibition. A book designed to relay the facts and the controversies that continue to form the substance of the way in which we imagine these wonderful animals. But, above all, it is a thoughtfully constructed book that portrays dinosaurs as living, successful animals, that were only different in appearance to the animals that live today. This book teaches us that dinosaurs were different only because they evolved unfamiliar adaptations to cope with the situations of life. They were not slow, stupid failures of evolution, but instead, the success story of their time.

John R. Horner

Curator of Paleontology, Museum of the Rockies, Bozeman, Montana, USA

February, 1993

THE DINOSA

I Dinosaurs are one of the great success stories of evolution, utterly dominating the land for 160 million years. Yet though they inhabited a world very different from our own, they had much in common with today's animals. Living in balanced communities, they faced the same survival needs — to breed, to feed, to hunt and escape their enemies.

T he Earth is constantly changing. Its climate, the shape of seas and continents, even the position of the magnetic pole have all changed many times during its 4600 million year history. These changes have determined the evolution of life, creating an environment that favors some plants and animals more than others. For a while the favored life forms thrive and diversify, while other, less adaptable forms die out. Then the environment changes again and new forms of life take over the planet.

It used to be thought that these changes weeded out the weaker life forms and allowed the better ones to press ahead in a constantly improving march of progress. The phrase "survival of the fittest" best sums up this idea. In fact, the surviving forms of life are only "better" in the sense that they can cope with the environmental changes the Earth throws at them. At its simplest, if the climate turns cold, animals with fur stay warm and do better than those without any insulation. Yet fur is not "better" than scaly skin, just useful in different conditions.

Dinosaurs have suffered particularly badly from the "survival of the fittest" prejudice. The fact that they became extinct was seen as proof that they were not "fit" to survive. They were too big, too slow and too stupid. This is wrong on two counts. Firstly, not all dinosaurs were big, slow and stupid. There were plenty of small, fast, clever ones as well. More significantly, although dinosaurs eventually did become extinct, they survived for a huge span of time — 165 million years — more than forty times longer than Man has so far achieved. Indeed, to say that they survived does not do justice to their evolutionary achievement. The fossil evidence clearly shows that, while they were alive, every land habitat worth having was occupied by some kind of dinosaur. Flying reptiles, and later birds, were able to colonize the air where the dinosaurs could not reach them. Huge marine reptiles swam in the dinosaur-free seas, but on land, with very few exceptions, no animal larger than a domestic cat ever managed to evolve while the dinosaurs were around. The early mammals, which are our ancient ancestors and whose superior intellectual powers we hear so much about, were mostly rat-sized creatures that scuttled about at night when the dinosaurs were safely asleep. Dinosaurs utterly dominated the land in a way that no other group of animals had done before.

In this book we set out to celebrate the dinosaurs' success and, as far as possible, to explain it. This means looking at dinosaurs not simply as giant monsters or complex skeletons, or even as fascinating twigs on a family tree, but as real live animals in a real environment, as members of a balanced animal community facing the same survival needs as today's animals — to breed, to grow, to eat, and avoid being eaten.

THE EVIDENCE
We have two main sources of information. The first is the fossil record — the physical evidence of the dinosaurs' existence left behind in rocks

HOW ARE FOSSILS FORMED? Dinosaur dies and is rapidly covered with waterborne sediment. Sediment compresses and hardens. Minerals seep through the bones, which gradually change into rock. Millions of years later the fossil appears as the covering rock is worn away by wind and water.

(Previous spread) SURVIVAL OF THE FITTEST. Three Deinonychus attack a solitary plant-eating Tenontosaurus that has unwisely strayed from its herd.

around the world. The word fossil comes from the Latin *fossilis*, meaning "dug up," and originally meant anything that was taken out of the ground, including minerals and crystals. Today, a fossil means the traces of any past life preserved in the rocks.

Despite surviving for so long, dinosaurs represent only a small fraction of the fossils found on Earth. Usually when an animal dies its body is rapidly destroyed. Scavengers tear pieces off and carry them away, the flesh rots, the skeleton falls apart, the bones disintegrate, and within a few weeks there is no recognizable trace. If the body is quickly covered with some sort of sediment, however, this process of disintegration may not occur. A desert sandstorm could do this, or mud on the banks of a river. If the dead animal fell into deep water or was washed into a lake, then the silt at the bottom could quite quickly cover it over. This is why by far the most numerous fossils are those of sea animals, particularly those that lived in shallow water near the coast, where mud and silt were constantly present to bury their dead remains. It is also why the bodies of dinosaurs (all land animals) very seldom became fossilized. It took unusual circumstances for the bones of a dinosaur to avoid the common fate of scattering and destruction. However, some dinosaur remains were covered rapidly and then turned into fossils in a number of different ways.

Once it had died and the sediment had covered it, the flesh and other soft parts of the dinosaur almost always rotted away, leaving only hard bones and teeth behind. Gradually, the sediment built up on top of the bones, compacting into rock such as limestone, mudstone, sandstone, clay, or shale. As this happened, minerals from water percolating through the surrounding rocks seeped into the bone structure, impregnating the tiny spaces and often altering the original mineral in the bone. These fossils, part original bone and part rock, are called "petrified."

Sometimes acidic water in the ground dissolved the bone and left a hollow mold where it used to be. These are "natural mold" fossils and, by pouring material such as plaster of Paris or rubber latex into them, the precise shape of the bone that used to be there can be created. In other cases, these natural molds filled later with sediments or quite different minerals such as silica, calcite or iron pyrites which gradually built up a perfect replica, creating a "natural cast" fossil. The rarest fossil of all formed when the dinosaur's body had been covered in a dry environment and some of the soft parts had become mummified and then fossilized.

In these fossils the texture of the skin, and even the folds in it, can be clearly seen. The color is not preserved, however, since the surrounding rocks give their own color to the fossil.

In addition, there is a wide range of other fossils, not actual dinosaur remains but evidence of their presence and their way of life (what a police officer would call "scene of crime" evidence). These include fossilized footprints or trackways, nests and eggs, scratches in the ground, tooth marks on bones, fossilized dung, stomach stones, and much more besides.

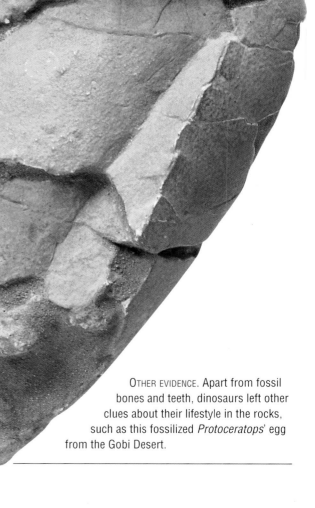

OTHER EVIDENCE. Apart from fossil bones and teeth, dinosaurs left other clues about their lifestyle in the rocks, such as this fossilized *Protoceratops'* egg from the Gobi Desert.

TRACKS AND TRAILS. Footprints and trackways tell us whether dinosaurs lived alone or in groups, and how fast they moved.

Taken together, all these direct and indirect remains make up the fossil record — the hard evidence (literally) on which our knowledge of dinosaurs as living animals is built.

The other major source of information about dinosaurs is observation of animals alive today. It is no accident that the first dinosaur scientists were also the world's leading experts on comparative anatomy, the study of animal structure to determine relationships between species. Their knowledge of animal anatomy allowed them to see the similarity between dinosaurs and some living creatures such as birds, lizards, and mammals. They could also appreciate the difference of scale that made the dinosaurs so extraordinary. So today's animals are an essential point of reference. This not only covers basic issues such as how dinosaurs stood and walked, but also questions about their behavior, their communication, their color, and their techniques for hunting and defense. Throughout this book we will be comparing what we know about dinosaurs with observations from our modern world.

Where did dinosaurs come from? That apparently simple question has been the subject of intense debate amongst scientists for over 150 years, and even today there are widely differing views about the origin of dinosaurs.

Life had been present on Earth for at least 3260 million years before the dinosaurs put in an appearance. Starting with simple one-celled organisms, over hundreds of millions of years the sea came to swarm with a huge variety of animals including worms, jellyfish, shelled mollusks, and later, fish with bony skeletons. The land was also gradually colonized, first by simple single-celled plants such as algae, and later by more complex plants and by animals — worms, arthropods (insects, scorpions, mites, and others), and mollusks. One group of bony fishes, the lobe-fins, which had lungs and strong fins with bony internal supports, began to venture on to land about 370 million years ago. These pioneers were the ancestors of both land-dwelling amphibians and the early reptiles.

By 245–235 million years ago there were many groups of reptiles living on the land. These included mammal-like reptiles that gave rise to mammals, rhynchosaurs (plant-eaters with curved beaks and strong digging hind feet), and archosaurs (the "ruling reptiles"). The earliest archosaurs, informally known as thecodontians or "socket-toothed animals," were all meat-eaters. Some were large crocodile-like animals with sprawling legs. Others developed a semi-sprawling stance and a special rotary ankle joint. This meant that they usually moved with their legs bent at right-angles at the elbow and knee, but were able to run over short distances with

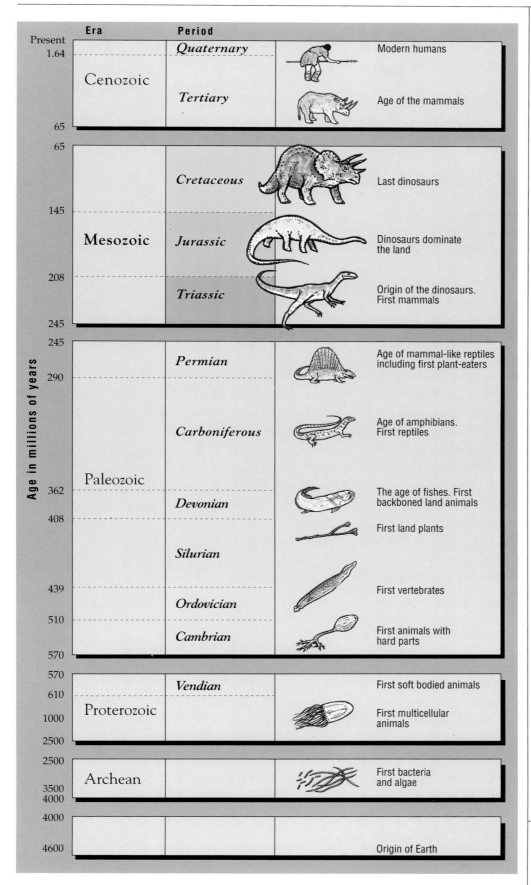

Age in millions of years	Era	Period	Notes
Present 1.64	Cenozoic	Quaternary	Modern humans
65	Cenozoic	Tertiary	Age of the mammals
65 – 145	Mesozoic	Cretaceous	Last dinosaurs
145 – 208	Mesozoic	Jurassic	Dinosaurs dominate the land
208 – 245	Mesozoic	Triassic	Origin of the dinosaurs. First mammals
245 – 290	Paleozoic	Permian	Age of mammal-like reptiles including first plant-eaters
290 – 362	Paleozoic	Carboniferous	Age of amphibians. First reptiles
362 – 408	Paleozoic	Devonian	The age of fishes. First backboned land animals
408 – 439	Paleozoic	Silurian	First land plants
439 – 510	Paleozoic	Ordovician	First vertebrates
510 – 570	Paleozoic	Cambrian	First animals with hard parts
570 – 610	Proterozoic	Vendian	First soft bodied animals
610 – 2500	Proterozoic		First multicellular animals
2500 – 4000	Archean		First bacteria and algae
4000 – 4600			Origin of Earth

their legs almost straight (modern crocodiles are their descendants). Smaller, lightly-built thecodontians were the first animals to develop the ability to run for short distances on their back legs and for some this became the fully improved stance, with straight legs permanently tucked under their bodies. The little 12 inch long thecodontian *Lagosuchus* from Argentina stood on the anatomical boundary between these improved stance thecodontians and the two groups that evolved from them — the flying reptiles (pterosaurs) and the dinosaurs themselves.

The dinosaur era, officially known as the Mesozoic Era, is divided into three parts called the Triassic, Jurassic, and Cretaceous Periods. These divisions do not really have anything to do with the evolution of the dinosaurs themselves, which carried on developing undisturbed between one period and the next, but relate to the different ages of rock where their fossils are found. The three periods are, however, essential reference points for dinosaur scientists, who usually talk about the early, middle, or late part of each to define when a particular dinosaur lived. During the Mesozoic Era the Earth and its environment underwent changes that had a profound effect on how dinosaurs evolved.

THE TRIASSIC PERIOD
In the Triassic Period (248–213 million years ago), all the continents on Earth were joined in one giant land mass. Called Pangaea (meaning "All Earth"),

IN THE BEGINNING. . . Dinosaurs evolved over millions of years from earlier life forms. Their nearest living relatives today are birds and crocodiles.

STEPS ON THE WAY. Early archosaurs with sprawling gait (1) gave rise to semi-improved walkers with rotary ankles (2). Small, lightly-built archosaurs like *Lagosuchus* (3) developed a fully upright stance and became bipedal. They gave rise to the earliest dinosaurs such as *Herrerasaurus* (4).

this supercontinent straddled the equator. The temperature on land stayed constantly warm and, with no polar ice-caps or large inland seas to affect the climate, there was very little seasonal variation, although it became hotter and drier toward the end of the Triassic. There seems to have been quite a difference in the plant life between the north and south of Pangaea although scientists are not clear as to the reasons why this should be so.

Because Pangaea was a single continent the dinosaurs were able to spread across it quite freely. Fossil remains of similar kinds are found in different parts of the world. The very earliest dinosaurs were small, slightly built, two-legged meat-eaters like *Coelophysis* (also recently known as *Rioarribasaurus*) and *Herrerasaurus*. These quite primitive dinosaurs, up to 10 feet long, were swift and vicious with sharp, pointed teeth and grasping claws. The first plant-eating dinosaurs also appeared at this time in the shape of prosauropods like *Massospondylus* and *Plateosaurus* which could walk on two or four legs, presumably rearing up to get at higher vegetation. Their fossil remains are very widespread, so their efficient digestive system was obviously able to cope with the differing plant life that spread across Pangaea. Although nowhere near the size of the later giant plant-eaters, the prosauropods were by far the largest land

WHAT IS A DINOSAUR?

Dinosaurs lived between 230–65 million years ago. Dinosaurs lived on land but could not fly. Dinosaurs had straight legs tucked underneath their bodies. Dinosaurs were reptiles. Which of these animals was a dinosaur? (Answers on next page.)

THE TRIASSIC LANDSCAPE. The dinosaur world in Europe around 210 million years ago. Giant horsetails grew in wetter areas, tree ferns and bennettitaleans were common, and tall conifer trees grew in drier areas.

THE JURASSIC LANDSCAPE. The dinosaur world in East Africa around 150 million years ago. Extensive fern land and forests of tall conifer trees such as sequoias and monkey puzzles dominated the lush tropical landscape.

THE CRETACEOUS LANDSCAPE. The dinosaur world in western North America around 70 million years ago. Flowering trees and shrubs, similar to beeches, oaks, grapes and hickory, grew alongside cycads, conifers and ferns.

animals of their time (*Plateosaurus* was up to 26 feet long), and an early example of how some dinosaurs used their sheer size to make themselves immune from attack.

The rise of the dinosaurs during the late Triassic led inevitably to the decline of other animal groups that had been very successful previously. Many of the sprawling reptiles and amphibians disappeared, as did the advanced mammal-like reptiles. Among the species that cohabited with the dinosaurs were insects of many kinds (often food for small and baby dinosaurs), crocodiles, and very small mammals. In freshwater rivers and lakes there was an abundance of life with frogs, turtles, and fish, but it seems unlikely that many of these were hunted by dinosaurs. Gliding lizards and the first pterosaurs took to the air and in the sea swam a variety of reptiles like ichthyosaurs and protorosaurs.

The late Triassic can best be seen as a period of colonization by the dinosaurs as they spread over the whole Pangaea supercontinent, replacing the existing inhabitants. Obviously the dinosaurs' superior mobility and speed played an important part in this, although some

A CHANGING WORLD. *Top:* Triassic. All continents joined in the single land mass of Pangaea. *Middle:* Jurassic. Two supercontinents of Laurasia (north) and Gondwana (south). *Bottom:* Cretaceous. Supercontinents continue to move apart and break up, and the land outlines come to resemble those we recognize today.
KEY: yellow = land; light blue = shallow seas covering continental shelves; dark blue = deep oceans.

WHAT IS A DINOSAUR ?

The Dinosaurs	The Non-Dinosaurs
6. *Brachiosaurus* — dinosaur.	4. Plesiosaur — non-dinosaur; lived in the seas.
10. *Deinonychus* — dinosaur.	1. Crocodile — non-dinosaur; did not have straight legs.
3. *Tyrannosaurus* — dinosaur.	7. Pterosaur — non-dinosaur; flew in the air.
8. *Chasmosaurus* — dinosaur.	2. Mammal-like reptile — non-dinosaur; lived 300 million years ago.
5. *Polacanthus* — dinosaur.	9. Ichthyosaur — non-dinosaur, lived in the seas.

scientists believe that climate changes may have caused many species to become extinct, leaving a gap in the ecosystem which the dinosaurs were able to fill.

THE JURASSIC PERIOD

In the Jurassic Period (213–145 million years ago), the single land mass of Pangaea was split in two by huge rifts in the Earth's surface that created two new land areas, Laurasia in the north and Gondwana in the south. Despite this dramatic separation, fossil skeletons of *Brachiosaurus* and plated stegosaurs are now found as far apart as Africa and North America, showing that there must have been at least occasional land bridges between the new supercontinents.

The break up of the land mass and the creation of large seas between the supercontinents affected the global climate. The temperatures fell slightly and increasing rainfall and a mild climate allowed lush tropical vegetation to grow over huge areas. Ferns and horsetails provided ground cover, while ginkgoes and tree ferns were found near many rivers and lakes. Some of this vegetation became coal seams which we still mine today. Forests of cycads, conifers and sequoias covered thousands of square miles of the drier areas.

The lush conditions gave rise to quite new and extraordinary kinds of dinosaur, among them the sauropods like *Apatosaurus*, *Diplodocus* and *Brachiosaurus*, the largest animals ever to walk on Earth. Anything that needs to consume a ton of greenery a day has to be sure of a huge supply within easy walking distance (you cannot waste good eating time trekking from place to place). The sauropods' long necks gave them access to the higher, treetop vegetation that other dinosaurs could not reach, and by the end of the Jurassic their herds dominated the landscape. Other new types of dinosaurs evolved alongside the sauropods, including the large meat-eaters like *Allosaurus* and plated plant-eaters like *Stegosaurus*. Smaller coelurosaurs like *Coelurus* and *Ornitholestes* hunted lizards, mammals, frogs, and insects among the ferns, horsetails, and mosses.

Apart from flying insects, including early ancestors of bees and flies, the air was dominated by the pterosaurs — the flying reptiles from the same original archosaur group as the dinosaurs. *Archaeopteryx* also appeared in the Jurassic Period. This is the earliest known bird and retains many distinctive dinosaur features, proving that birds actually evolved from small meat-eating dinosaurs.

In terms of sheer size and geographical spread, the Jurassic Period is the high point of the dinosaur era. The fully improved stance, so effective in giving the early dinosaurs an evolutionary lead over the other archosaurs, also allowed them to develop varied body shapes and sizes to exploit different parts of the ecosystem. By the end of the Jurassic, dinosaurs had expanded to fill virtually every usable part of the land surface. Increasing numbers of the largest sauropods roamed in herds and trampled large areas of vegetation.

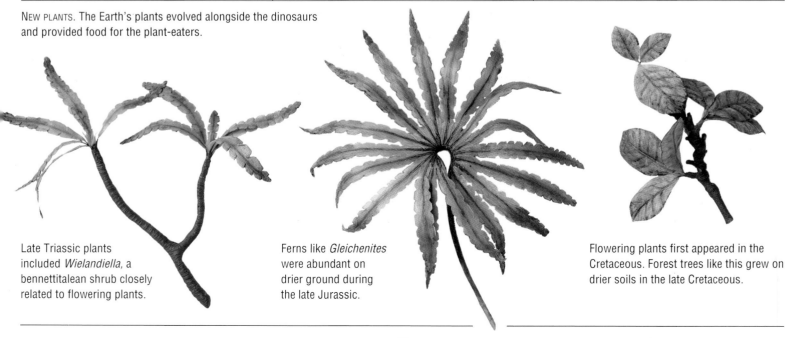

NEW PLANTS. The Earth's plants evolved alongside the dinosaurs and provided food for the plant-eaters.

Late Triassic plants included *Wielandiella,* a bennettitalean shrub closely related to flowering plants.

Ferns like *Gleichenites* were abundant on drier ground during the late Jurassic.

Flowering plants first appeared in the Cretaceous. Forest trees like this grew on drier soils in the late Cretaceous.

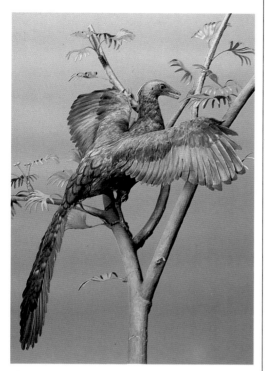

THE EARLIEST BIRD. *Archaeopteryx,* the earliest known bird, found in Germany in rocks which are 147 million years old, shows a mixture of reptile and bird features (*opposite and above*). These include a reptile-like bony tail and claws on the fingers, as well as feathers and a "wishbone" which are characteristic of birds. The skeletons of *Archaeopteryx* and some small meat-eating dinosaurs show so many similarities that most palaeontologists agree that birds are their descendants. So birds are the dinosaurs' closest living relatives.

THE CRETACEOUS PERIOD

The two supercontinents of Laurasia and Gondwana continued to move apart during the Cretaceous Period (145–65 million years ago), and by the end of that period the outlines of continents were roughly those that we recognize today. The early Cretaceous climate was warm with wet and dry seasons. Later, more pronounced summer and winter seasons developed, although the temperature probably never dropped below freezing even in the polar regions.

The biggest single environmental change during this time was the appearance of flowering plants (angiosperms). It may be that trampling of slow growing plants by large dinosaur herds in the late Jurassic was the key to the rapid spread of the angiosperms, which grow back very rapidly when they are trampled down (ask any gardener). Their seeds would have been easily dispersed by wind, insects, and passing dinosaurs. Starting as small herbs, they came to be the dominant plant group, virtually replacing the ferns and horsetails with a dense ground cover of small flowering plants, bushes, and trailing stems. They also formed large forests and woodlands of deciduous trees.

The combined effect of the land breakup and the new plant life had a direct effect on the development of the dinosaurs throughout the Cretaceous Period. Because there were fewer land bridges, dinosaur populations on each of the continents remained isolated from each other (this had already begun to happen in some areas like Australia). There came to be very noticeable differences between the species developing in each area — the North American hadrosaurs and the equivalent groups in China or Africa are a good example of this. Indeed, in China and Mongolia recent disoveries of strange meat-eaters like *Segnosaurus* and the peculiar-looking *Oviraptor* seem to show that entire groups existed here that were not found anywhere else. In Europe, covered by a continental sea and divided into large islands, this local specialization took an even more extreme form with the evolution of dwarf versions of larger dinosaurs such as the small iguanodontids *Rhabdodon* and *Craspedodon* and the miniature armored dinosaur *Struthiosaurus.* Many kinds of animals that we would recognize today first appeared in the Cretaceous Period. These included snakes, some birds, and moths. The flying reptiles continued to develop and the largest of these were the biggest animals ever to take to the air. *Quetzalcoatlus,* for example, had a wing span of up to 36 feet, about the same as a World War II fighter.

The best exposed area of late Cretaceous fossil-bearing rock is found in western North America. Here the fast-growing flowering plants created great dinosaur ranges that were able to support huge herds of plant-eaters such as *Triceratops, Kritosaurus* and *Parasaurolophus.* The bones of up to 10,000 plant-eaters of the same species have been found in one area, giving an indication of just how extensive these herds were. Preying on the plentiful supply of meat were the great carnosaurs such as *Albertosaurus* and *Tyrannosaurus* and smaller scavengers such as *Troodon* and *Dromeosaurus.* These would also have attacked the many smaller plant-eaters in the region. And yet the picture here is only a local one and this pattern of dinosaur life was not repeated elsewhere in the world. Indeed, the development of such different local dinosaur populations makes it difficult to draw many general conclusions about the dinosaur world at this time.

What is certainly true is that we know of more different species from the late Cretaceous than from all the other dinosaur periods put together. This part of the dinosaur era was the highpoint of their development in terms of variety and sheer numbers. The fact that these huge populations of different animals were all wiped out at the end of the Cretaceous remains one of the greatest mysteries of dinosaur sciencé.

GETTING

2 One of the keys to the dinosaurs' success was their way of walking upright on straight legs. This gave them an advantage over other animal groups, which were sprawling

ABOUT

walkers, and later allowed them to adopt a wide range of lifestyles. Plodding giants, huge hunters, roaming herds and swift-footed scavengers each evolved their own variation of walking upright.

Dinosaurs walked with straight legs tucked underneath their bodies. It was this ability, never achieved by any other reptile before or since, that opened the way to the evolution of a variety of body types and lifestyles. This helped them to become the dominant land animals and remain so for 160 million years.

Four-legged land animals with a backbone (vertebral column) walk in one of three ways. A lizard sprawls with legs held at right angles to its body. Forward movement is achieved by throwing its weight from side to side and moving its legs one at a time. A crocodile also sprawls most of the time but can sprint for short distances with its legs nearly straight and its body lifted off the ground. This is called the semi-improved stance. All mammals and birds have a fully improved stance, with legs held straight under the body at all times, whether walking, running, galloping, or hopping. Humans walk like this and so did dinosaurs.

There are many advantages to the fully improved stance. You do not have to drag your body along the ground to walk like the lizard does, or use huge amounts of energy throwing your weight about. The wrist and ankle joints of sprawlers, and even semi-improved walkers, also have to withstand great twisting and pulling as the animal moves. Nothing very big could walk in this way, putting a severe limitation on the way that such a species can evolve.

Recent research also suggests that sprawling makes it difficult to breathe and move at the same time, the constant body bending interfering with the lungs' action. Fully improved walkers do not have this problem. The dinosaurs achieved what is called "locomotor stamina," and this ability to run and breathe at the same time ultimately gave them a huge advantage over the sprawlers.

Having a fully improved stance allows an animal to grow bigger, walk further, and move faster, and this opens the evolutionary path to a huge range of body types and lifestyles. This can be clearly seen with today's fully improved walkers, birds and mammals — some are huge, some fast, some tall, some agile. The dinosaurs too, having once achieved fully improved walking, evolved to exploit it in many different ways.

A PLODDING GIANT

The large sauropods like *Diplodocus* used the fully improved stance to develop to a huge size, so large that a fully grown adult could not be attacked by any predator. Some remarkable physical adaptations were required to achieve such bulk. *Diplodocus* stood on four thick, widely spaced legs. These supported its huge shoulder bones and hip girdle, rather like pillars holding up the cross beams of a building. The five vertebrae across the hip were actually fused together to form a strengthened support for a hip girdle that could take the immense pressure of an 11 ton body on the move. All four legs ended in short, broad feet rather like an elephant's. *Diplodocus'* front toes were probably rounded horny pads, but the inner toe on the front foot had a much longer, sharper claw. There were sharp claws on the three inner toes of the back foot as well and these were probably an anti-slip device, able to dig into soft ground and prevent *Diplodocus* from skidding or getting stuck at the bottom of a slope.

Diplodocus and other sauropods also had built-in "high heels." When you walk you raise your ankle at each stride to lift your whole body weight. This is actually quite tiring and the reason why shoes with heels make walking easier. If lifting a 150 pound human an inch above the ground at each stride is hard work, imagine the energy cost to an 11 ton *Diplodocus*. Elephants have the same problem today, and have solved it by growing a thick

(*Previous spread*) A GIANT AFLOAT. One set of dinosaur trackways seems to show *Apatosaurus* walking on its front feet only! Scientists have concluded that it was floating in water, pushing itself along with its front feet and steering with the back legs.

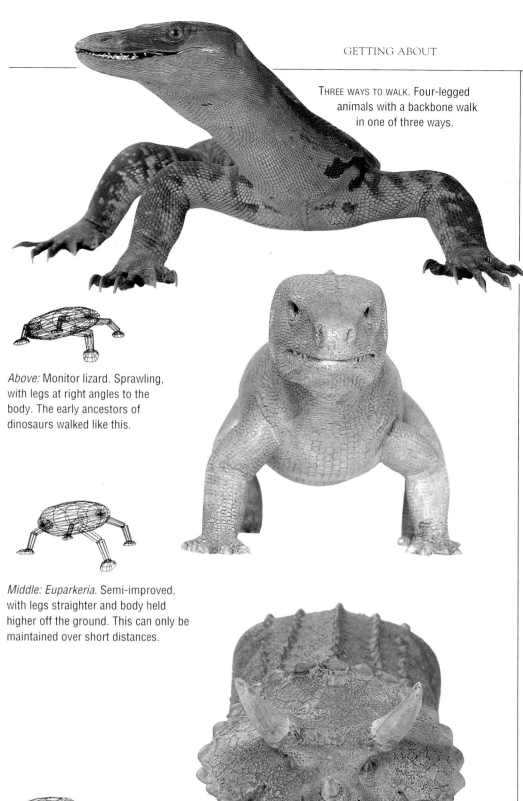

THREE WAYS TO WALK. Four-legged
animals with a backbone walk
in one of three ways.

Above: Monitor lizard. Sprawling,
with legs at right angles to the
body. The early ancestors of
dinosaurs walked like this.

Middle: Euparkeria. Semi-improved,
with legs straighter and body held
higher off the ground. This can only be
maintained over short distances.

Right: Triceratops. Fully improved,
with straight legs tucked under the body.
The upright stance was the key to the
dinosaurs' success.

wedge of fibrous tissue under the heel of each foot. The same solution worked equally well for the sauropods.

Although quite a few sauropod trackways have been found around the world, there are very few that show evidence of tail-drag marks. We can only conclude that *Diplodocus* and the other sauropods kept their tails up off the ground when they walked — a sensible arrangement, since a heavy tail would soon get worn down to the bone after a few miles on the move. This would have been achieved by large hawserlike ligaments which ran along the tail and attached to the top of the hips. Similar ligaments ran all the way down the sauropods' long necks, through V-shaped guide tracks in the tops of the spines of the back vertebrae, also attaching to the hip area. These two sets of ligaments worked together, allowing the weight of the neck and tail to balance each other and keeping both off the ground.

Being on the move was not a speedy business for this group of dinosaurs. As far as we can tell from their physical structure and the trackways they left behind, most sauropods moved at about 4 mph — human walking pace. Perhaps, like elephants, they were capable of modest bursts of speed, but the forces of torque and compression on their bones and tendons would have been hugely increased by even a gentle trot, so they must have conducted most of their lives at a gentle amble.

The extraordinary size of the sauropods gave rise to some bizarre theories, in the early days of dinosaur study, about how they moved. Until quite recently some scientists believed that an animal as huge as *Brachiosaurus* could never have

VARIATIONS ON A THEME. Today's land animals show how versatile the improved stance can be, supporting many different body types and methods of moving. The elephant is a heavy, slow moving quadruped; the ostrich is a fast bipedal runner; the cheetah runs very fast on all four legs; the polar bear can walk on two legs as well as on all fours. Dinosaurs exploited the improved stance in similar ways.

BUILT FOR SIZE. *Diplodocus'* skeleton shows how the improved stance was used to support huge weight. The legs were like pillars holding up the cross beams of shoulders and hips. Ligaments ran from one end of the spine to the other, keeping the head and tail up without wasting energy.

supported its own body weight on land and must have lived in the water. The fact that all sauropods had nostrils on the tops of their heads was seen as further evidence of this. In fact, *Brachiosaurus* had a physique that was quite capable of supporting itself on land; the pressure exerted on its lungs if it had been submerged in water would have meant instant death. Even earlier, when dinosaurs were still thought of as huge lizards, the sauropods were said by some German scientists to have had sprawling legs and to have rested their huge bodies on the ground. The discoverers of the original *Diplodocus* in America, however, showed that the dinosaur would have needed a 6 feet deep pit underneath its belly to stand in this position, and a network of trench runways to move about! These early mistakes are an indication of just how extraordinarily different the sauropods were from any living animal and how difficult scientists found it to understand them. Today we can see the sauropods as the supreme example of what the improved stance made possible for dinosaurs in terms of sheer bulk on an evolutionary path that sacrificed everything to size.

A DINOSAUR SPRINTER
At the other end of the scale, *Hypsilophodon* shows how the fully improved stance allowed the development of impressive speed and agility. *Hypsilophodon* was a two-legged plant-eater standing just 5 feet high. Many well-preserved skeletons have been found in one location on the Isle of Wight, England, where at least twenty-five *Hypsilophodon* died together, possibly after wandering into an area of quicksand. The most striking feature about a *Hypsilophodon* skeleton is how

EARLY THEORIES. *Top:* Early dinosaur scientists thought that the largest dinosaurs like *Brachiosaurus* could only have moved when buoyed up by water. *Bottom:* The idea of a sprawling *Diplodocus* was also popular at one time. But how could it have moved with its belly hanging below ground level?

little there is of it. Rather like a gazelle or antelope, the whole structure had been slimmed down to give maximum support for minimum weight. Even the bones themselves were thin walled and

hollow, just like a gazelle's. The thigh bone of *Hypsilophodon* is quite short, allowing it to be pulled rapidly back and forth for fast strides. The foot, by contrast, is remarkably long and thin, with very elongated upper foot bones (metatarsals), and thin toes ending in short, sharp claws. This structure gave a very flexible grip on the ground and could sustain long periods of fast running. The completely defenseless *Hypsilophodon* must have made frequent use of its speed to escape its enemies, helped by its long tail, stiffened by bony rods. With *Hypsilophodon* in its typical horizontal running posture, the tail could have been swung from side to side for rapid changes of direction without stopping.

Like the sauropods, *Hypsilophodon*'s way of moving was considerably misunderstood when it was first discovered. Scientists assumed that the big toe on its foot actually faced the opposite way from the other toes, rather like a bird's. *Hypsilophodon*, they said, must have been a tree dweller, perching in the branches and using its tail to balance, just as the Australian tree kangaroo does. In fact, as we now know, *Hypsilophodon* shows how the fully improved stance enabled quite small, unarmored dinosaurs to thrive by developing high levels of speed and maneuverability to escape their enemies.

TWO OR FOUR LEGS
While *Diplodocus* was a four-legged walker and *Hypsilophodon* a two-legged one, there were some dinosaurs that could move in both ways, rather like modern bears. Using two and four legs gave these dinosaurs several advantages. They could rear up and use their hands for gripping food or doing battle with an

BUILT FOR SPEED. *Hypsilophodon* had the light, slender skeleton of a fast runner.

Hypsilophodon's large, strong leg-moving muscles were concentrated on the thigh and hip to allow the long, lower leg to swing fast through a long stride.

The upper foot bones were long and the lower foot thin and flexible, very like today's running birds.

STRIDING OUT. This computer generated picture shows the stride patterns of *Hypsilophodon*, a fast runner with a long stride.

enemy, for example, as well as browsing for low-level food on all fours. They could rest or walk slowly about with all four legs on the ground, but if a sudden increase of speed was required, they could hoist up on two legs and get away.

Iguanodon is one of the best known examples of a dinosaur that exploited the fully improved stance in this way. Related quite closely to *Hypsilophodon*, *Iguanodon* was built on a much larger scale with a fully grown adult reaching up to 33 feet in length and weighing 4 tons. Its skeleton had exactly the same basic structure as *Hypsilophodon* but the proportions of the bones were very different. The thigh bone was heavy and long and the upper foot quite short, giving great strength to carry the weight of the body, but no real ability to run. The spines on the vertebrae were much wider and taller, with numerous bony tendons criss-crossing along their whole length to give added strength without the weight of extra muscles. Since *Iguanodon*'s first discovery there has been much debate about just how it held its body in the normal walking stance. Horizontal like a lizard? Upright like a kangaroo? Most

A PERCHING DINOSAUR? *Hypsilophodon*'s foot skeleton was once thought to show that this dinosaur was a tree dweller, similar to the Australian tree kangaroo (*above*). *Right:* This model shows the mistaken idea.

scientists now agree that a fully grown adult *Iguanodon* probably walked with a nearly horizontal spine, allowing the back legs to take most of the weight but dropping down frequently on to all fours for extra support when feeding or standing around.

Iguanodon's arms were one of its most remarkable features and show again how very adaptable the improved stance was for the dinosaurs. Supported by huge shoulder bones, the arms were long, powerful and heavily muscled. The five bones of its wrist (carpals) were fused together to give a strong inflexible support, very different from *Hypsilophodon*'s sliding wrist bones. The three middle fingers were strong and stiff, ending in short, blunt claws that

TWO AND FOUR LEGS. *Left:* Bony tendons all along the spine gave *Iguanodon* strength and support. *Right: Iguanodon* was able to walk upright and on all fours.

would have splayed out like hooves during four-legged walking. The thumb was a fearsome spike, *Iguanodon*'s main weapon when it reared up on its hind legs in defense. The fifth finger was weaker than the others but much more flexible, and could have been used as a hook to pull down food from the trees.

THE BIG HUNTERS

Of all the dinosaurs it has been the large meat-eaters like *Albertosaurus* and *Tyrannosaurus* whose means of getting about has caused most dispute among scientists. There is general agreement that they had the fully improved stance,

ADVANCED HANDLING. *Left: Iguanodon* had an extraordinarily multipurpose hand. The thumb carried a large spike for self-defense while the three middle fingers would have splayed out like hooves for four-legged walking. The flexible fifth finger could grasp food and strip leaves from the trees.

THUMB SPIKE. *Iguanodon* rears up to lash back at an attacking allosaur with its thumb spike. The fully improved stance allowed *Iguanodon* great freedom of movement.

that they were two-legged and grew to a great size (up to 7 tons for an adult *Tyrannosaurus*). Beyond this point agreement ends, with one group seeing them as slow and lumbering scavengers and another as speedy hunters. Both groups often interpret the same evidence to reach quite different conclusions, and the whole subject is a good reminder of how little we actually know for certain about many aspects of dinosaurs.

As with all dinosaurs, study begins with the skeleton. In the case of *Tyrannosaurus* this was huge and heavy with particularly massive vertebrae, hip girdle and thigh bones to anchor the muscles and tendons that controlled movement. The metatarsal bones of the upper foot were actually locked together to make an extraordinarily strong pillar of bone. The three toes that took its weight were short and powerful, ending in large claws. At first sight this does not look like the body of a fast runner. The slow movement group say that the sheer can get up to speeds of 22 mph over short distances.

The theropods' knees are another area that both groups believe prove their own case. Dinosaurs' knee joints were similar to yours, a rollerlike hinge shaped to allow forward and backward movement without twisting. In modern mammals the bone ends are highly ossified (bony) with a very thin cap of softer cartilage to allow smooth movement of the joint. Dinosaurs, on the other hand,

show evidence of having had pads of much thicker cartilage between the ends of their upper and lower limb bones. This is similar to today's juvenile birds, as you can clearly see should you have a chicken for dinner. This cartilage, say the slow moving enthusiasts, would have been unable to take the shock of a running theropod and was designed to allow the animal to move at a slow plod. Not so, say the fast movers. Cartilage is an ideal material for fast running since it spreads the weight over the whole joint and provides a smooth lubrication for the knee as it moves back and forth.

Trackways are another source of controversy. Literally thousands of meat-eater trackways have been found around the world, some belonging to the largest species. They demonstrate, among other things, that these large meat-eaters seldom traveled in groups, that they walked almost on tiptoe and probably had a slightly bow-legged stance to keep their feet directly underneath them without their knees hitting their own large bellies at each stride. What they do not prove is whether they could run, because all the trackways so far discovered have been of walking animals. This is because they never ran, say the slow moving advocates. The fast moving group point out that most modern animals, including some of the fastest,

SPRINTING OR LUMBERING? Does this view of a large theropod suggest a fast or slow animal? The *Tyrannosaurus* skeleton is heavy and does not suggest a fast mover but the upper foot bones are locked together for strength, possibly to withstand the stresses of running, indicating that perhaps it was indeed a fast-moving animal.

weight of flesh and bone would have prevented sprinting, and that the stresses imposed on the bones by running would have been fatal to an animal of this size. The advocates of fast movement disagree, suggesting that the bulk of muscle and bones would only have developed if *Tyrannosaurus* had used them for running. They point out that some bones are capable of taking the same stresses as mild steel, around 1000 lb/in^2, and that large modern animals like the rhinoceros spend most of their lives walking and that running trackways are therefore very rare.

However, the fact that none have been found does not mean they do not exist.

For the moment, with the direct evidence still in dispute, our conclusions about the big theropod's movement must rest on deduction. *Tyrannosaurus* was a huge meat-eater and hence required huge quantities of meat. It would be unlikely to find this lying around as carrion, so it must also have hunted. Unless it was a master of ambush and disguise it must have been able to move at least as fast as its prey, outrunning hadrosaurs like *Edmontosaurus* and ceratopians like *Triceratops*. Some of these dinosaurs are believed to have been able to reach 9–12 mph at top speed (and running away from a large meat-eater would definitely justify top speed), so *Tyrannosaurus* may have been able to do the same over very short distances. A sustainable running speed of around 6 mph for *Tyrannosaurus* seems much more likely, although a smaller meat-eater such as *Scartopus* (actually known only from its tracks) might have reached nearly 10 mph in hot pursuit.

The large meat-eaters show yet another adaptation of the fully improved stance, combining bulk with a hunter's speed and power. So successful was this adaptation, in fact, that they became the largest hunters ever to live on Earth, a clear testimony to the effectiveness of the fully improved stance as an evolutionary pathway.

FOOTPRINTS IN THE ROCK

Trackways are obviously important in understanding dinosaur movement but occasionally a set of trackways can reveal much more information, even a complete incident from the prehistoric world. One such set has been found at Lark Quarry in Australia and is thought to show a dinosaur stampede.

The trackways date from the Lower Cretaceous Period and probably form part of the dried-up bed of a small stream or river that was still muddy enough to take an impression of footprints. The preserved section covers 2250 ft^2, running from north to south, and probably led down to a waterhole, all traces of which have now disappeared. From the trackway evidence we get a picture of about 150 small meat-eating and plant-eating dinosaurs gathered around this waterhole. Presumably the plant-eaters were there in sufficient numbers to prevent an attack by the meat-eaters, but both groups must have been keeping a wary eye on each other and on the surrounding countryside.

From the northern end of the

MUSCLE POWER.
The huge sheets of muscle on the legs of *Albertosaurus*, closely related to *Tyrannosaurus*, were certainly strong enough to achieve considerable speed over short distances.

HUNTING REPTILE. Although usually a slow mover, the Komodo dragon can run at up to 9–11 mph in pursuit of prey. The big theropod dinosaurs must also have been able to move at least as fast as their prey.

TRACKWAY EVIDENCE. *Above:* A track from Lark Quarry showing the smaller dinosaurs' footprints covering that of the big hunter.
STAMPEDE! *Right:* This computer reconstruction shows the Lark Quarry trackways and the sequence of events that may have happened. *Top:* Smaller dinosaurs gather at the water course. *Middle (×2):* Large meat-eater approaches from northern end. Smaller dinosaurs stampede back past the hunter. *Bottom:* The hunter closes in on escaping small dinosaurs, and a mass of large and small trackways are left behind.

watercourse there appears a large meat-eating dinosaur, standing 8.5 feet at the hip, which advances four paces. The footprints then suggest a change of tempo, almost as if it was here that the hunter spotted the group of smaller prey. The stride becomes shorter and the foot pad impressions disappear as it moves forward on tiptoe for five further steps and then turns. Some time in these final few seconds the small dinosaurs at the waterhole see the hunter. There is instant panic as all of them stampede back toward it. Why toward? It is impossible to say. Perhaps the waterhole was, in fact, a wide lake that cut off their retreat. Perhaps another meat-eater was stalking them from the opposite direction. In any case, the whole group (less any that the hunter picked off on the way past) charged back up the watercourse, covering it with the footprints that we can see today.

Dinosaur locomotion is important because it was vital to their success. In the early stages of their evolution it was the only thing that distinguished them from the many other animals that could have become dominant on land. Later on, its energy efficiency and above all its versatility set the dinosaurs on an evolutionary track more spectacularly diverse and successful than any group of land animals had ever achieved before. Dinosaur diversity has been surpassed only by that of the mammals which eventually replaced them. Mammals include burrowers, fliers, and swimmers — dinosaurs never went underground, took to the air, or became aquatic.

FOOD AN

3 As with all today's animals, the base of the dinosaur "food chain" was plants and the species that ate them. These provided meat for the hunters and scavengers that preyed on herds or individual victims. Some dinosaurs also developed remarkable specialist equipment, such as grasping hands, swivelling claws, and grinding teeth, to catch and process their food.

Animals either eat plants or each other. A plant-eater's food is not hard to catch (being literally rooted to the spot) but can be very hard work to process and digest. This is because plants are largely composed of cellulose, a chemical compound that is difficult to break down. If a plant-eater is to get enough nutrition, it needs a complex food processing system. Meat-eaters have a much easier task getting energy from their food. Animal flesh and fat are both energy rich and break down rapidly under the action of digestive acids and enzymes. The meat-eaters' problems lie in catching their food, which tends to run away or fight back, and eating it quickly before it turns rotten and poisonous.

Most dinosaurs can be divided clearly into plant-eaters and meat-eaters. The equipment they used to obtain and process their food is well known as far as jaws and teeth are concerned, and we can tell fairly accurately from the fossil record what there was around to be eaten (see Chapter 1: The Dinosaur World). Beyond these facts there is much less certainty. After all, it is precisely soft internal organs like the stomach and gut that are the first to rot away when an animal dies, and no part of a dinosaur's digestive system has ever been found as a fossil. We must rely instead on deduction from the fossil evidence and the application of modern animal dynamics.

A TON A DAY

The biggest dinosaurs of all were the plant-eating sauropods of the Jurassic Period. To obtain enough nutritional energy to keep their bodies going, these giants must have consumed vast quantities of plants. The nearest modern equivalent would be the African elephant, which must eat around 410 pounds of plants every day to survive, over 3 percent of its own body weight. At this rate, a 30 ton *Brachiosaurus* might have chomped through around a ton of vegetation per day. Yet all this consumption was achieved with a head less than 30 inches long, not very much larger than a horse's, and teeth which did no chewing at all.

For many years the sauropods' small heads and teeth convinced scientists that they could only have survived on a diet of aquatic plants. *Diplodocus*, for example, had just a short row of pencil-thin teeth at the front of its mouth. With such equipment, it was said, only the softest waterweed soup could

CHOP AND RAKE. *Left:* These robust chopping teeth from *Pelorosaurus*, a sauropod, show where the outer enamel has been worn away by constant chopping at plants. *Opposite:* The slender, pencil-thin teeth of *Diplodocus* would have raked leaves from the branches. *Diplodocus*' nostrils were on top of its head, possibly to avoid being spiked by stray twigs when feeding.

(Previous spread) A HUGE HUNTER. A lone-hunting *Allosaurus* makes a savage assault on a young *Diplodocus*. The victim will provide food for several days.

possibly have been processed in sufficient quantities to keep it alive. Yet why should the sauropods develop such extremely long necks, up to 36 feet in the case of *Mamenchisaurus*, if they were only going to use them for water-level browsing? It seems most likely that the sauropods were mainly treetop browsers and their long necks were for reaching high trees where, as

any giraffe will tell you, the leaves are tender and no other animal can get at them.

Yet even if sauropods' lives were one long meal among the treetops, how were such huge quantities of food processed, particularly in the absence of chewing teeth? The answer lies in the rounded pebbles that are occasionally found at sauropod fossil sites. These pebbles (called gastroliths) are polished, smooth, and made of quite different material from the surrounding rocks. They come from the gizzards of sauropods and were a vital part of their eating equipment.

The best modern comparison is a bird's gizzard. A strong muscular sack, the gizzard is the second part of a bird's stomach which it fills by swallowing grit or small stones. Food passes through the bird's first, glandular stomach into the gizzard where muscular action grinds the stones together like a gastric mill, reducing the food to a thick paste. This is then sent on to be further broken down by bacteria and the nutrition extracted. A gizzard is a very good way of dealing with all kinds of tough material. Ducks can crush clam shells with theirs, while the tropical fruit pigeon's gizzard cracks the toughest nuts and seeds. This is how the big sauropods managed to process their daily ton of plants, saving themselves the bother of chewing. Their gizzards, perhaps similar in structure to those of some birds, would have worked effectively on anything they found in their treetop browsing, and certainly not restricted them to a diet of soft water plants.

If today's animals are anything to go by, dinosaurs may well have been very choosy about where they obtained their gastroliths. Many birds prefer the hardest rocks available, such as quartz which wears down slowly, and will travel for long distances to find the right sort. Some of the gastroliths from dinosaur fossil sites also originated many miles from where the dinosaur actually died. One *Massospondylus* skeleton found in Zimbabwe had gastroliths that came from at least 12 miles away.

It is certain that the big dinosaurs would have got through a lot of gastroliths in the course of a year's eating. A specimen of the North American *Barosaurus* was found with sixty-four polished stones between its ribs. When a bird's

STONE CRUSHERS. Modern birds have gizzards, a muscular part of the stomach in which small stones or grit crush up the food before it reaches the intestines. Dinosaur stomach stones (gastroliths) have been found near, and sometimes actually inside, the ribs of sauropods and parrot dinosaurs.

gastroliths become too smooth to work properly it belches them up and takes new ones on board. It is entertaining, although probably fanciful, to speculate about a peaceful dinosaur landscape rent asunder by whizzing gastroliths regurgitated at high velocity by hungry sauropods.

CHOPPING AND GRINDING

For plant-eating dinosaurs without gizzards it was teeth and jaws that had to crush and shred the food for the digestive system, just as with modern grazing and browsing mammals. All these dinosaurs had grinding or chewing teeth, but two in particular demonstrate how effectively different groups adapted to take advantage of particular kinds of food.

Edmontosaurus was a herding hadrosaur from the Upper Cretaceous Period. By this stage the dominant ferns, cycads and horsetails of the earlier dinosaur periods had been overtaken by the flowering trees and bushes. Tough leafed conifers of various kinds were also common. *Edmontosaurus* had a wide, flat beak covered in horn that cut or pulled at the vegetation. Its powerful tongue would then push the food back toward the multiple rows of cheek teeth, called tooth batteries, where an extraordinary grating and grinding process took place. The upper teeth fitted neatly over the outside of the lower teeth to give two interlocking grinding surfaces. The teeth were constantly replaced by new ones growing up underneath so the tooth battery was always being renewed. On their own these would have been impressive chewing equipment, but there were a number of additional refinements that made *Edmontosaurus* a particularly efficient eater.

First, it had cheeks as did almost all other plant-eating dinosaurs. This may seem a small achievement, but no modern reptile has them, which makes them relatively inefficient eaters. When a land turtle chops a blade of grass, at least half falls from each side of its mouth on to the ground. *Edmontosaurus'* efficient chewing would have been useless without muscular cheeks to hold the food in place. The second feature was the rough, graterlike surfaces of the tooth batteries. This developed because the hard outer enamel of each tooth wore away more slowly than the softer core of dentine, giving a pattern of dips and ridges that could shred the toughest greenery. Finally, the whole upper jaw of *Edmontosaurus* was specially hinged for chewing. When humans chew, our lower jaws swing slightly from side to side with each bite to let the back molars grind against each other. In *Edmontosaurus* the upper jaw moved slightly outward on both sides, hinged by great sheets of muscle just below the eyes. The pressure of the closing lower jaw pushed the upper jaws out sideways so that the upper and lower tooth batteries could shred and crush at the same time. Analysis of the stomach contents of exceptionally well-preserved fossils shows that hadrosaurs ate, among other plant material, bark, pine cones, branches, and the toughest kind of conifer needles — food that no other dinosaurs could handle. As with *Brachiosaurus* in the high branches, this left *Edmontosaurus* and its relatives as

TOOTH BATTERY. Two views of the lower jaw of a plant-eater.

The teeth worked together as a single graterlike surface which ground up the toughest plants.

the unchallenged owners of a specialized area of food supply.

A very different kind of food specialization was developed by *Protoceratops* and the other horned dinosaurs. At the front of their mouths a sharp, narrow beak sliced off the chosen shoots and leaves. Further back the scissorlike tooth batteries operated a fine cutting action, chopping but not grinding the food before it was swallowed. This system was well suited to dealing with tough, low-growing fibrous plants such as palms and cycads which *Protoceratops* may have eaten.

Brachiosaurus, *Edmontosaurus* and *Protoceratops* show three different strategies that plant-eaters can adopt to compete effectively for food — special access, special processing, and specialized

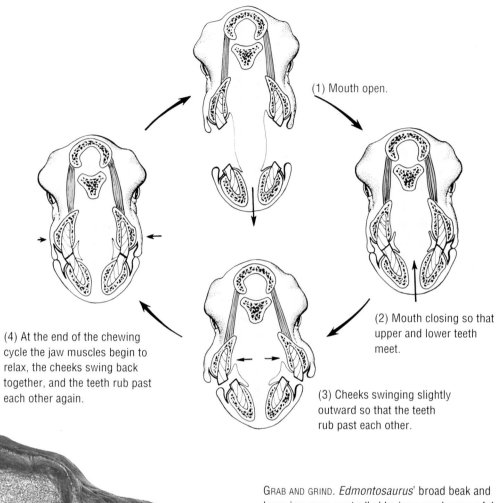

CHEWING ACTION. This face-on view of *Edmontosaurus* shows its chewing cycle.

(1) Mouth open.

(2) Mouth closing so that upper and lower teeth meet.

(3) Cheeks swinging slightly outward so that the teeth rub past each other.

(4) At the end of the chewing cycle the jaw muscles begin to relax, the cheeks swing back together, and the teeth rub past each other again.

GRAB AND GRIND. *Edmontosaurus*' broad beak and large jaw were controlled by immensely powerful chewing muscles. The jaws contained up to 1000 teeth arranged in upper and lower batteries.

selection. The shape of the mouth is often a good indication of which strategy a dinosaur primarily adopted. Ankylosaurs like *Euoplocephalus*, for example, had the very wide, flat mouths of generalized eaters and presumably did not discriminate much between one branch and the next after they went to work on a bush. Small ornithopods like *Hypsilophodon*, with its very narrow mouth, would have been able to choose exactly which leaves to accept and which to reject. Modern animals operate in just the same way. The African buffalo's wide jaw is designed to do a quite different job from the narrow one of the antelope, even though they feed on

exactly the same areas of land.

The shape of some dinosaur mouths is so specialized that we still do not know exactly what they were used for. The jaws of *Oviraptor*, for example, were probably covered by a horny sheath like a bird's beak. The mouth had no teeth at all but there were two bony toothlike projections in the roof of its mouth. The lower jaw was also curved to give an extremely powerful bite. Did it use these to crush and feast on the eggs of other dinosaurs? The first specimen ever discovered was just above a nest of *Protoceratops* eggs, giving the dinosaur its name, which means "egg thief." Some modern animals, such as snakes, weasels, and birds, do steal eggs but few survive on a diet of eggs alone — there simply are not enough to be found. If this was indeed how *Oviraptor* fed, it suggests

that lots of dinosaur nests lay unprotected all the year round. Other suggestions are that it dug up mollusks in shallow water and crunched their shells between the powerful jaws or that it cracked open hard fruits or seeds. Whatever the true reason, *Oviraptor*'s unique mouth must have given it access to some kind of food that no other dinosaur could eat.

DEADLY TEETH AND JAWS
The life of a meat-eating animal is very different from that of a plant-eater. When a deer wakes up in the morning it can be pretty certain that the grass will still be there, it is just a case of standing up and starting to nibble. A plant-eater's life, and particularly the life of a plant-eating dinosaur, was really a continuous process of eating with short breaks to sleep, breed, squabble, and move on to the next patch of greenery. The meat-eater has no regular food supply, and any meal it does catch may have to last for several days. Most modern meat-eaters, especially big hunters, actually spend most of their time resting (twenty

CLIP AND CHOP. *Protoceratops* could use its beak for selective feeding, just as a parrot does. Self-sharpening teeth at the back of the mouth then cut up the plants with a scissorlike action.

hours sleep out of twenty-four for male lions) with occasional huge bursts of energy for hunting. They gorge themselves on a kill, taking in up to 25 percent of their own body weight at one feed, and then rest until hunger drives them out to hunt once more. The big meat-eating dinosaurs must surely have followed a similar pattern.

When a big meat-eater like *Allosaurus* went hunting it would head for the herding grounds of *Diplodocus*, *Apatosaurus* and *Camptosaurus*. With luck, it might find the remains of a carcass on the way or a group of smaller meat-eaters gathered round a fresh kill. Few hunters will waste energy on pursuit and killing if some other animal has done the work for them, and all the large meat-eaters were probably occasional scavengers, eating carrion or stealing from smaller dinosaurs as the opportunity arose.

Indeed, some scientists believe that the really huge tyrannosaurs from the end of the dinosaur era were not actually hunters at all but superscavengers. Among today's animals the only pure scavengers of any size, who do no hunting at all, are vultures and condors. They achieve this by being able to survey huge areas of land from the air, spotting newly dead and dying animals dozens of miles away. Obviously the tyrannosaurs had no such ability, so if they were to survive on carrion alone it suggests that there must have been a very large number of dead dinosaurs to satisfy their monster appetites. This question raises some of the most basic issues about the large meat-eating dinosaurs — whether they were warm- or cold-blooded and therefore require

NARROW MOUTHS. Narrow mouths allow animals to select food with more care like this kudo. *Hypsilophodon* would have been able to pick out soft shoots and leaves.

BROAD MOUTHS. A wide mouth usually shows a generalized feeder like this cape buffalo, with the emphasis on quantity rather than quality. Ankylosaurs' broad, shovellike mouths were designed to work in this way.

EGG HEAD. *Oviraptor*'s jaw was designed to exert great pressure, just as the modern parrot uses its curved beak to crush tropical nuts *(opposite)*. Did *Oviraptor* use the spikes in the roof of its mouth to break open dinosaur eggs and feast on their energy-rich contents, or did it too feed on hard fruit or perhaps even shellfish?

more or less food, whether their monumental teeth and jaws would have evolved for scavenging alone, and (as we saw in the previous chapter) whether their physiques would ever have allowed them to move fast enough to be effective hunters. All these ideas are hotly debated by dinosaur experts.

Allosaurus is definitely a hunter, and a very hungry one by the time it spots a herd of *Diplodocus* browsing on the tree tops (see pages 32–33). It is looking for a vulnerable member of the herd to attack — old, young, sick, or disabled are all suitable. *Allosaurus*, like lions or leopards, must have been skilled at spotting the signs of weakness or the subtle changes in the herd pattern that showed one member beginning to stray. Most of hunting is watching and waiting, and *Allosaurus* might shadow the herd for several hours. Hunting alone, it would be essential to stay out of sight, for once the adult *Diplodocus* spotted danger they would instantly gather into a defensive formation, easily able to see off a single predator and possibly inflict fatal damage with their whiplash tails.

Suddenly the moment arrives. One young *Diplodocus* has lagged behind the herd and is now far enough away to risk an attack. *Allosaurus* breaks cover and moves forward, putting itself between the juvenile and the herd. At the sight of the hunter the young *Diplodocus* makes a dash to get back to its parents. Being small, it might be able to outrun the *Allosaurus*, but the hunter is already roaring and edging closer, causing the *Diplodocus* to panic, turn, and run. The chase that follows is not long or fast. Neither of these dinosaurs was built for speed and the combined effects of fear and fatigue would soon cause the *Diplodocus* to slow to a terrified standstill.

SLASH AND TEAR. *Allosaurus* had about sixty curved, daggerlike teeth to kill and dismember its prey. Serrations on the front and back edges made for effective meat-slicing action, while hinged jaws allowed large pieces to be swallowed whole.

NEW FOR OLD. Teeth were replaced throughout the animal's life as they wore down or broke. This *Megalosaurus* jaw shows new teeth growing up on the inside of the old ones.

The scientific term for what happens next is macropredation. The *Allosaurus* opens its mouth to the furthest extent and runs headlong at its victim. The daggerlike teeth, driven onward by 2 tons of dinosaur, plunge into the young *Diplodocus*. Its struggles to escape only help the teeth slice further in with their sharp serrations on the front and back edges. *Allosaurus* holds the victim with its front claws and begins to close its jaw, tugging in a series of rapid jerks with its powerful neck. As a chunk of flesh comes away, *Allosaurus* raises its head and swallows the piece whole. The *Diplodocus* may still be alive but the first priority is to eat the meat as fast as possible. The gorging goes on, with each mouthful torn from the carcass and swallowed whole without any chewing. The front claws, which were much more powerful than those of the later *Tyrannosaurus*, could be used to tear pieces off the carcass. Finally, having consumed a huge quantity of meat, the *Allosaurus* moves off to find a safe spot to rest. There will be no need to hunt again for several days.

Hunters like *Allosaurus* and *Tyrannosaurus* are comparatively rare in the fossil record. Smaller meat-eaters range from the fearsome *Deinonychus* (whose possible pack hunting habits are described in Chapter 5), to the speedy *Compsognathus* which stood no higher than a hen. The smallest meat-eaters must have hunted lizards, mammals, and large insects. For smaller meat-eaters, insects represent highly concentrated packages of nutritional energy. Indeed, the juveniles of many modern reptiles start on a diet of insects until they are big and fast enough to capture other prey, so perhaps juvenile dinosaurs did

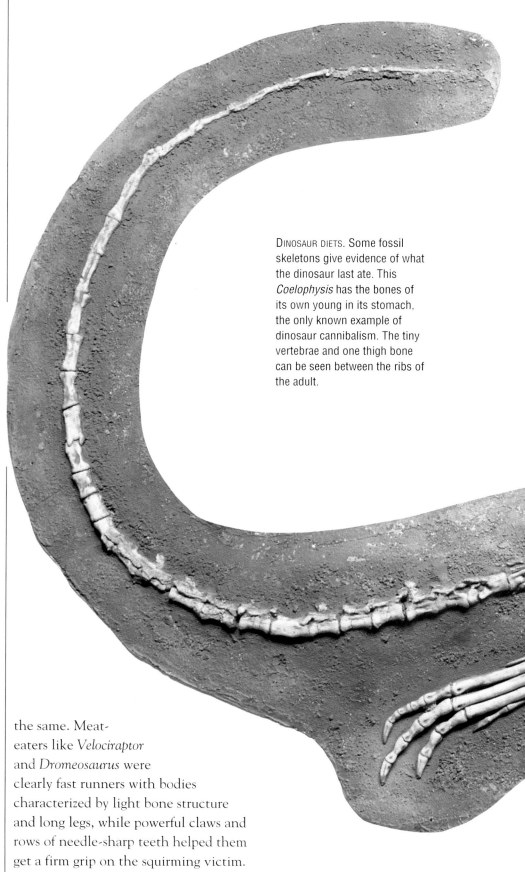

DINOSAUR DIETS. Some fossil skeletons give evidence of what the dinosaur last ate. This *Coelophysis* has the bones of its own young in its stomach, the only known example of dinosaur cannibalism. The tiny vertebrae and one thigh bone can be seen between the ribs of the adult.

the same. Meat-eaters like *Velociraptor* and *Dromeosaurus* were clearly fast runners with bodies characterized by light bone structure and long legs, while powerful claws and rows of needle-sharp teeth helped them get a firm grip on the squirming victim.

It is not possible to deduce from the evidence currently available what sort of hunting each of these many meat-eaters specialized in. Particular refinements of their anatomies do give clues and occasionally a fossil skeleton is found with the remains of the dinosaur's last meal still inside. Thus we know, for example, that *Coelophysis* was a cannibal, since the bones of several babies have been found inside the stomach of an adult.

Compsognathus from Germany was discovered with the half-digested remains of a speedy lizard called *Bavarisaurus*, while the recently discovered British dinosaur *Baryonyx* was found to contain scales and teeth of the large, nonmarine fish *Lepidotes*, making it the only known fish-eating dinosaur.

The ability to obtain and process food is key to any animal's survival and a major factor in determining its evolutionary development. The dinosaurs were overwhelmingly dominant on land and grew in some cases to an enormous size. These facts alone are a tribute to how efficiently they managed to exploit the available food supply and turn virtually every land habitat into a potential feeding ground.

ATTACK AN

Just like the animals of today, dinosaurs attacked each other, defended themselves and competed for leadership within groups. The equipment they used was sometimes spectacular and lethal, yet for every giant hunter like *Tyrannosaurus* there were many more small plant-eating dinosaurs which did nothing more aggressive than running away.

The largest hunter ever to walk the Earth was *Tyrannosaurus*. A pack of *Velociraptor* could have ripped a human being to pieces in 30 seconds and *Allosaurus* could have swallowed you in two mouthfuls. Yet the dinosaur world was not actually dominated by roaming gangs of monster killers. Most dinosaurs were peaceful, plant-eating creatures that never attacked anything in their lives. The weapons they carried were either used to defend themselves or to compete for food, space, and a mate within their own group. And while it is the attackers that usually make headlines in dinosaur books, the defenders and competitors were just as spectacular in their own right.

Modern animals have many ways to defend themselves — disguise, running away, herding together, fighting back. Strategies range from the active use of teeth, claws, and horns to passive weapons like camouflage and armor. One dinosaur with a remarkable combination of active and passive defenses was *Euoplocephalus*.

CLUBS AND ARMOR

Euoplocephalus was a four-legged plant-eater, cropping low growing vegetation of the North American ranges with its toothless beak. Every part of its back, neck and tail was armored with bony plates set into the skin. These varied from huge blunt spikes and slabs across the neck and shoulders, down to thousands of pebble-sized lumps like chain-mail along the tail. The head was even more heavily armored, with slabs of reinforcing bone over all exposed surfaces and triangular side studs above and below the eyes. The very eyelids themselves were made of bone, closing like steel shutters to deflect the gouging claw of an attacker.

Euoplocephalus' passive defense strategy was simple. Crouching down to protect its soft belly, it presented a completely armored shell, with every part of the body protected. No amount of slashing or biting could make any real impression, and the only option for an attacker was to try and flip *Euoplocephalus* over on its back — about as hard as overturning a 2 ton slab of rock, particularly when its front legs were "locked" into a defensive position against its shoulders.

Despite the huge weight of all this armor, perhaps half a ton in all, *Euoplocephalus* seems to have been surprisingly agile. Muscle scars round the hips and shoulders suggest it had enormously strong legs which gave mobility as well as controlling the movement of a giant tail club. For, while armor provided passive protection, *Euoplocephalus* also had a devastating active defense weapon that could transform it from a frustratingly

WEAPONS AND THEIR USES. Attack, defense, and competition are keys to any animal's survival. *Top:* Hunters combine speed and strength with weapons that kill quickly. *Middle:* Tough armor provides excellent passive defense for an armadillo. *Bottom:* Bighorn sheep butt heads in the mating season. This is more bluff and display than real fighting.

(*Previous spread*) A KILLER EYE. Any dinosaur that got this close to a *Tyrannosaurus rex* probably never saw anything else again.

inaccessible meal into a highly dangerous adversary.

The tail of a fully grown *Euoplocephalus* was around 8 feet long and ended in a huge club made of two fused bones weighing up to 66 pounds. By lashing out from side to side, the club could deliver a scything blow to the legs, easily enough to smash bones or send the largest tyrannosaur crashing to the ground. Once down with a broken shin or worse, the attacker never rose again and soon fell victim to other hunters and scavengers on the prowl. In its active defense stance we can imagine *Euoplocephalus* being circled by a wary tyrannosaur, looking for an opening for the quick hind leg kick that might tip the smaller dinosaur over or disable it. All the time *Euoplocephalus* circles as well, turning its back toward the attacker with tail poised to strike. It would be a very confident or a very hungry hunter indeed that felt like taking on such an opponent.

DEFENSE AND COMPETITION
For large sauropod dinosaurs like

OFFENSIVE WEAPON. A tyrannosaur circles a *Euoplocephalus*. One blow from the tail club could be fatal.

Brachiosaurus, size alone was usually sufficient defense. As with elephants today, there were no predators large enough to tackle a fully grown adult. All sauropods also had a pair of thumb spikes. In the case of the rather smaller *Diplodocus* these could perhaps have been brandished while it reared up backward, leaning on its tail. The tail itself was also a formidable whiplash weapon — equivalent to 43 feet of flailing telephone pole.

At the other end of the scale, the skeletons of small plant-eaters such as *Dryosaurus* show that running away was often the best form of defense. Good hearing and eyesight must also have been essential for rapid flight at the first sign of danger.

BUILT FOR DEFENSE: *Euoplocephalus*.

(1) Bony eyelid.
(2) Bone plates protect top and side of head.
(3) Triangular bony plates above eye.

(5) Ribs and hips welded together anchor the massive hind leg and tail-swinging muscles.
(6) Extra bony tendons stiffen tail to prevent "whiplash" damage as club is swung.
(7) Huge bony tail club weighing up to 66 pounds.

(4) Short front legs give a low, broad posture.

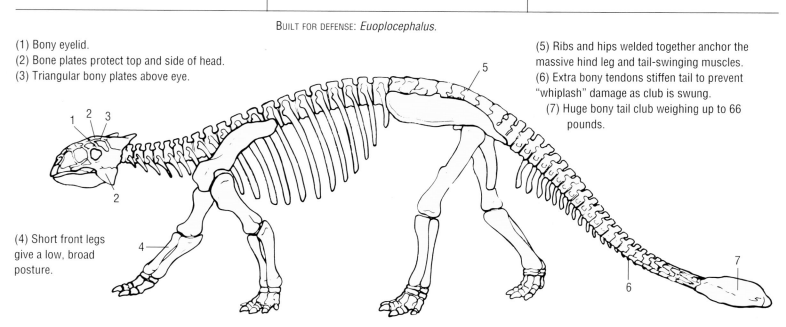

Diplodocus' claw and tail, *Dryosaurus'* speed and the armor on *Euoplocephalus* are highly developed versions of defense strategies found extensively throughout the dinosaur world. Plant-eaters would usually have tried to escape before fighting. Many protected vulnerable parts of their bodies, such as necks and spines, with bony neck frills, tooth-snapping bone studs, and plates, and many had a sharp claw, horn, or spike for swift counterattack. For dinosaurs, like today's animals, defense did not usually mean being totally immune from any attack but slightly harder to catch or to kill than other prey nearby. A balance of active and passive defenses to keep one step ahead, sometimes literally, was the way that most dinosaurs developed.

Dinosaurs that lived in herds for protection would almost certainly have competed with each other. Many gregarious and social animals operate within a firm social structure. Whether it is apes or insects, there must be a clear mechanism to fix the function of every member (leaders, followers, and partners) if the group is to survive. Sometimes this mechanism is genetically programmed in the animal, but in other cases social order is determined by competition between group members. The strongest elephant leads the herd, the smartest looking peacock gets a mate. Such competition, even if it involves actual fighting, very seldom results in death or serious injury. The purpose, after all, is to establish order in the group, not reduce its overall strength. Many herding dinosaurs had features, such as crests or bony frills, that suggest social hierarchy. In one case, however, the competitive feature is so remarkably developed that the dinosaur is actually named after it, *Pachycephalosaurus*, the "thick headed lizard."

Pachycephalosaurus was a two-legged plant-eater that lived in western North America during the late Cretaceous Period. At first glance it looks like a dinosaur genius. Surely that high domed head housed a mighty brain! But no, the head was solid bone, up to 10 inches thick, providing protection for a brain no bigger than a tennis ball. Protection from what? From the crunching impact of a head butting contest with another *Pachycephalosaurus* as they did battle to establish social order within the herd.

The evidence for this activity lies chiefly in the structure of the skull and spine of *Pachycephalosaurus'* smaller relatives from North America and Asia. The off-center way that the head met the neck allowed the animal to adopt a head-down charging position when walking or running. Strong ligaments joined the skull to the back of the neck, absorbing the shock and transferring it to the spine. The spine itself was strengthened with bony rods and had a special grooved joint between each vertebra to prevent twisting under pressure. There may also have been air spaces around the brain to reduce the jolt it received. All this would have enabled two male *Pachycephalosaurus*, each as long as a bus, to hurtle together and clash heads at truly terrifying speed without doing fatal damage.

Probably all herding dinosaurs used noisy bluff, display, and trials of strength in

NATURAL COMPETITORS: Pachycephalosaurs.

(1) Neck and head joint allows a head-down running position.
(2) Special grooved joint prevents spine twisting under impact.
(3) Bony tendons stiffen spine to absorb impact of head butting.

HEAD TO HEAD. Two male *Pachycephalosaurus* crash heads in a leadership battle. Massively thick skulls protect their brains.

KILLED IN ACTION. This *Protoceratops* and *Velociraptor* from Mongolia are the only example of dinosaurs discovered in combat. The *Velociraptor*, its chest crushed, still had its claws gripped behind the enemy's neck frill. Just below the bodies was a nest of *Protoceratops*' eggs, so perhaps the *Velociraptor* was caught in the act of robbery. Both dinosaurs were overcome by a sandstorm as they fought, and died still locked together.

one way or another to organize themselves. For it was only in a coherent, well-ordered group, staying close to a leader, looking after their own family members, and swiftly following direction, that any herbivores could hope to survive the attentions of the many attackers that lay in wait for them.

A STREAMLINED KILLER

If any dinosaur deserves to be described as built for attack it is *Deinonychus*, a streamlined killer that combined agility and speed with ferocious weaponry. Standing about 6 feet tall and up to 9 feet long, *Deinonychus* had the light, long-legged physique of a fast runner. A sheath of bony rods along the tail made it stand out stiffly behind. This acted as a counterbalance when sprinting after a victim, giving extra maneuverability.

Deinonychus had a slim neck and lightweight skull, ideal for quick, snapping bites. Teeth were backwardly curved for efficient meat-slicing action, but were not actually the main killing weapon. The real power lay in its savage combination of front and hind claws. The arms acted as long grappling hooks, grabbing a small creature to keep it still or allowing *Deinonychus* to leap up and hang on to a larger dinosaur. The second claw on the hind foot was like a crescent-shaped slashing knife. One blow, delivered with a massive sweeping kick, would have been enough to rip open the belly of a victim or tear it in half. The whole foot was adapted to keep the big claw in good condition. When walking or running it was pulled up and back to avoid blunting on the ground. When attacking, it could swivel through 180° to find the best possible angle of entry.

When the first *Deinonychus* fossils were found in Montana in 1964, scientists noticed that there were the remains of several of the predators near the body of a much larger herbivore, *Tenontosaurus*. Did they hunt in groups? Certainly *Deinonychus*' brain was relatively large and probably well developed in the areas vital to a pack hunter, namely those of sight and sound. Bringing down a big dinosaur would have provided several days' food supply, even if it had to be shared.

The dinosaur era produced many fine hunters, but in *Deinonychus* we see the near perfect balance of an attacker's skills. Intelligence to stalk, ambush, or mount a co-ordinated attack, the speed to run a quarry down, and the weapons to kill and dismember it.

Many of the other meat-eating dinosaurs developed one of these qualities at the expense of the others. *Tyrannosaurus*, for example, depended on bulk and enormous strength to overpower its prey. Its head was heavily reinforced with bone and shock absorbing muscle to withstand the impact of crashing into a victim with mouth open and then delivering a crushing bite and neck twist. But with a body weight of 7 tons *Tyrannosaurus* had clearly sacrificed speed to size. If it did not catch its quarry in the first rush there was no question of setting off in a lengthy pursuit.

At the other end of the scale, *Troodon* developed speed and brain power at the expense of size and weaponry. A small, fleet-footed predator, *Troodon* had a

Bony rods stiffen tail to counterbalance while sprinting.

large brain and front facing, stereoscopic eyes, probably allowing it to stalk rat-sized mammals that came out at dusk, when other dinosaurs could not see to hunt.

Euoplocephalus, *Pachycephalosaurus*, and *Deinonychus* all bear the evidence of their way of life clearly written in their bones. Yet the fossil record tells us little about the attack and defense behavior of most dinosaurs and many fascinating questions remain unanswered. What use, for example, did they make of camouflage and disguise, so important in many modern animal communities?

CAMOUFLAGE

Well-preserved fossils of dinosaur skin are very rare but in some cases sections of the skin did become dried out and

FOSSILIZED *EDMONTOSAURUS* SKIN. A fragment shows tiny bony plates embedded in the surface, but no color.

ANATOMY OF A KILLER: *Deinonychus.*
The light, slenderly built skeleton
with long arms and legs was an
active and agile predator.

Sharp backward
curving teeth
for tearing flesh.

Long arms hold victim
in position for hind claw blow.

Powerful legs for speed
and leaping attacks.

Huge claw on second toe
swivels into kick slash
position and folds up
when running.

preserved,
perhaps because
the animal was
rapidly buried by a
sandstorm that hid it from
scavengers and mummified the body.
These scraps of evidence show that
dinosaurs were covered with tough,
scaly skin like modern reptiles. We know
that color helps modern animals to
conceal, disguise, and identify
themselves. With so many different
dinosaurs living in such varied habitats,
it seems certain that they too would
have used color in attack, defense and
competition.

A medium-sized hadrosaur like
Kritosaurus would have spent much of its
time browsing on ferns and low bushes

under the forest canopy.
A dappled skin color of
greens and yellows, like an
anaconda, would have been
ideal to camouflage its low body among
the sunsplashed vegetation on the
ground. When it sensed danger
Kritosaurus might well have frozen still,
just as bushbuck do, in order to blend
into the forest and remain unnoticed.
Parksosaurus, browsing in the same
forest, might perhaps have developed a
more definite skin pattern like a striped
monitor lizard to keep itself concealed as
it passed through broken areas of light
and shade.

Bold countershading is the disguise used
by the mainly nocturnal okapi browsing
in areas of dense undergrowth. The dark
back, and its striped and light rump and
upper/lower legs, serve to break up the
body shape when seen from a distance,
providing protection against predators
like leopards that hunt by sight. Perhaps
the fast moving hunter *Troodon* had

VARIED DISGUISE. An anaconda, okapi and monitor lizard show three modern approaches to the use of color in attack and defense. Do they give a clue to the way that dinosaurs like *Kritosaurus*, *Troodon*, and *Parksosaurus* may have looked?

similar coloring in order to conceal itself.

Color must also have played a key part in dinosaurs' competitive behavior. Many male animals today, particularly small birds and reptiles, adopt bright identifying colors during the mating season. The coloring announces that the male is ready to breed, helps females make their choice of partner, and can often be linked to clashes between competing males.

Perhaps crested hadrosaurs such as *Corythosaurus* and *Lambeosaurus* took on special head coloring as their herd approached its mating ground. *Saurolophus* and *Edmontosaurus* may have used their fleshy nose sacks rather as an elephant seal does to produce booming mating cries. Possibly the sack itself became brightly colored. The head structure of *Styracosaurus* also hints at display and competition. Its round bony frill was actually longer than the skull itself, and decorated round the outer edge with long spikes. Yet the frill was not solid bone like *Triceratops*', but contained two large openings covered with muscle and skin. By tilting its head forward and swinging it from side to side, *Styracosaurus* could produce an impressive display of size and aggression to frighten off other males and advertise its prowess. Two male *Styracosaurus* with horns locked like stags' antlers could engage in pushing, barging, and bellowing contests that

would produce spectacular and noisy proof of virility without any real injury being done. Once again, the skin coloring of the frill might have changed to a distinctive pattern at mating time.

Beyond the painstaking deduction based on firm fossil evidence, it is fascinating to speculate about the true behavior of dinosaurs in situations of attack, defense and competition and to imagine them as

vividly colored as today's birds and reptiles, their nearest living relatives. Yet speculation is all it can be. Future discoveries will undoubtedly provide more evidence about dinosaur lifestyles, and new techniques of laboratory analysis may fill gaps in our knowledge. But it is unlikely that we shall ever uncover all the dinosaur secrets. Some will remain forever buried in the rocks that entombed them millions of years ago.

HORNS AND SPIKES. *Styracosaurus* seen head-on would present a formidable sight to an attacker.

SOCIAL ORC

5 Social organization remains one of the great mysteries of dinosaur science. Yet, as living animals, they must have displayed patterns of behavior similar to those we see in

ANIZATION

today's animal colonies have world. Recent discoveries of nesting shown that some dinosaurs achieved a high level of social organization.

If any aspect of prehistory requires the use of a time machine, it is the study of dinosaurs' social lives. Biologists can spend many years with communities of lions, gorillas, or birds to observe how they live. Only such detailed fieldwork can give a true insight into complex family structures, group behavior, and techniques for survival. You cannot do much field observation on a fossil skeleton, so paleontologists must draw evidence from a wide range of sources to gain a picture of dinosaurs' social behavior.

The results are mostly speculative with the words "perhaps," "possibly," or "maybe" tending to appear in virtually every sentence. Some experts prefer to avoid this area of study altogether, yet dinosaurs were social animals operating in herds, packs, families, and at the very least mating pairs. They shared the same land — hunting and avoiding each other, competing for space and food, just as modern animals do. Social behavior is as important to understanding dinosaurs as looking at their bones and teeth under a microscope.

If we think of dinosaurs as members of a widely spread, balanced community, with each member dependent on the others, then the closest parallel in today's world are the African savannas. The foundation of these communities are the plants (grass in the savannas but *not* in the dinosaur world; see Chapter 1), which provide food for numerous plant-eaters. These in turn are food for the hunting meat-eaters that live near the fringes of their herds, catching what they can. It takes a lot of plant-eaters to support a meat-eater. One lion, for example, needs access to at least 100 gazelle or zebra to provide enough hunting opportunities for survival. Behind the hunters come the hyaenas and jackals, animals that often live off the leftovers of the big kills, and occasionally do some killing of their own, and the true scavengers such as vultures.

There are many levels of interdependence between these different animal groups. It is obvious that lions need zebra and gazelle to eat. It is less obvious, but equally true, that zebra and gazelle need lions to keep their numbers down and prevent huge herds from overgrazing the range and causing mass starvation. Elephants consume a huge amount of food each day, enough to feed scores of smaller oryx and wildebeeste. But oryx and wildebeeste need the elephants, whose amazingly destructive eating habits — uprooting and trampling — open up the forest for bush animals and the denser bush to plains dwellers. Antelopes share their grazing grounds with ostriches because ostriches are such good lookouts, and so on. In the dinosaur world too there must have been many such examples of interdependence between groups that chased, fled, avoided, or shared territory with each other.

THE LONE HUNTERS
Except in very rare cases, no skeletons of big hunting meat-eaters have been found near each other. This is in contrast to many "mass grave" finds of herds of plant-eaters, and suggests that some, at least, of the large hunters operated alone. This is good survival logic, since there is no point in cutting down your food supply by sharing a hunting ground with another large stomach. The carnosaurs would have had little to gain from cooperative hunting as they were so much bigger than many of their potential victims and would have needed no help to kill them. For a single hunter the best places are forests or dense scrub, since this gives plenty of opportunity for ambushing animals that would certainly spot you coming on a flat plain. The modern leopard uses this lone hunting technique.

There are some areas where the number of meat-eating dinosaur trackways, both large and small, is surprisingly high. These may have been favorite hunting spots, perhaps along the shores of rivers and lakes, where the hunters constantly patrolled to pick up carrion that drifted ashore, or attack plant-eaters as they came to drink.

However lonely a life the big hunting dinosaurs may have led, they must have got together to produce baby dinosaurs. Again, we have very little evidence of their mating habits, although eggs attributed to meat-eaters have recently come to light in the Gobi Desert. Did

(*Previous spread*) A NESTING COLONY. A colony of the hadrosaur *Maiasaura* looking after their young in the nest. The dinosaur's name means "good mother lizard."

they nest in groups or alone? One clue could be the discovery of different meat-eaters' skeletons with the bones of their own young inside their stomachs. Among today's animals, male bears and lions will occasionally try to kill off the young of other males, and some reptiles will actually eat their own hatchlings if put under stress. If cannibalism was part of the hunting dinosaurs' behavior they would have tended to nest alone. They might also have been female dominated with the male being kept well away from the nest by the aggressive mother, and even being seen off completely after successful mating. The hatchlings would probably have stayed with the parent, or parents, during their most vulnerable early months, eventually leaving to find their own territory. A tantalizing recent fossil find seems to show an adult *Tyrannosaurus* in association with a smaller adult, a juvenile, and a baby. This may prove to be the first evidence of a carnosaur family group.

LONE HUNTERS. Hunt alone like a leopard or *Tyrannosaurus* and you do not have to share the kill. A lone hunter must be strong enough to overwhelm its prey (here an unfortunate *Edmontosaurus*) and then keep other scavengers away from the carcass.

THE PACK HUNTERS

There is good reason to believe that some of the smaller meat-eating dinosaurs lived and hunted in packs. Cooperative hunting is practiced by many of today's animals with different degrees of sophistication. A surging army of soldier ants will make a concerted attack on a wasps' nest and destroy it with great efficiency. This is certainly cooperative, although the level of interaction it requires is pretty low. At a more complex level, pelicans fish together, and lions have complex techniques of encircling and stalking that may include several individuals operating as a highly organized team. The advantage of cooperative hunting is clear — the ability to get more and bigger prey than can be achieved alone. Some pack hunters can bring down a victim as large as their total combined weight. The disadvantage is having to share the kill, but even this is not necessarily very serious. With a whole pack feeding from a carcass very little goes to waste through rotting, and there is no need to defend the kill over a period of hours or days from the attentions of other scavengers as it is quickly devoured.

DINOSAUR HERDS. *Above:* Multiple trackways are evidence that some plant-eating dinosaurs lived and moved in large herds. This picture shows a herd of *Centrosaurus* in a defensive circle. *Right:* A mass grave of *Centrosaurus* shows where a herd crossed a swollen river and many individuals were swept away.

As mentioned in Chapter 4, the first find of the fossils of the meat-eater *Deinonychus* suggested that they might have been hunting in a pack to bring down a *Tenontosaurus*. How many were there in the group, and what hunting techniques did they use? It is easy to imagine several of them gripping onto *Tenontosaurus'* tail to slow it down while the pack leader leapt up to deliver slashing hind claw blows to the flank and stomach. Or did *Deinonychus* hunt in smaller, family-based groups?

Modern African hunting dogs give an indication of how effective such co-operative hunting can be. The degree of communication required to hunt together often extends into the complex social interaction between pack hunters. Before each hunt a highly ritualized series of sounds and movements binds the African hunting dog pack together, reinforces its social order and sends it on its way. They also share the spoils of the hunt with their young pups as well as old and sick members not able to join the chase. Pups old enough to run with the hunt are allowed to eat their fill before the adults finish off the carcass.

The social life of *Deinonychus* makes a tantalizing case study. There is just about enough evidence to place them as pack hunters. It is reasonable to assume that cooperative hunting was reflected in some form of cooperative lifestyle that encompassed mating, rearing young, migration, and movement as well as just attacking prey. Yet we are left with many unanswered questions. It is not until we come to the herding plant-eaters from the end of the dinosaur era that we start to find some really convincing proof of the complexities of dinosaurs' social behavior.

THE HERDING DINOSAURS
There have been enough discoveries of groups of skeletons together to be sure that the plant-eating hadrosaurs and ceratopians of North America lived and moved in large herds. Some of the finds are literally mass graves, with one "bone bed" in Alberta, Canada, containing the fossilized remains of at least 300

Centrosaurus of all sizes, from yearlings to large adults. The composition of the surrounding rocks suggests that there might have been a deep river in the area and the *Centrosaurus* herd was swept away trying to cross it. An even more extraordinary mass grave in Montana contains the bones of at least 10,000 *Maiasaura* whose herd was overcome by volcanic gases and buried in ash. The bed of preserved bones stretches in a solid line for more than a mile. Other mass finds are less spectacular but still clearly show members of the same group or species sharing land area, adults and young together. So it is reasonable to look at these particular dinosaurs for further evidence of family and group behavior.

Some hadrosaurs had varied head crests which invite comparison with the many different horn shapes of antelope in the African savannas. For these hadrosaurs, as for antelope, the fancy headgear had several uses. Its distinctive shape gave a means of instant recognition to members of the same species — very important if you need to move off with your herd in a hurry. Antelope horns also distinguish between male and female, and there is some evidence that hadrosaur crests did the same. Detailed measurement of the fifty or so crests so far found, shows that there were large and small versions within each species. Some hadrosaurs may also have been able to use their crests as sound making devices. Dr David Weishampel of Johns Hopkins University, Baltimore, has built a full-scale model of the long crest of *Parasaurolophus*, reproducing exactly the size and shape of the internal tubes. By blowing air through as *Parasaurolophus* would have done, the model produces a low note rather like an oboe. Such a sound, and variations on it, would give plenty of scope for communication and aggressive bellowing at mating time. It is also ideal for sounding the alarm to the herd when a predator is spotted. Low-frequency sounds offer two important advantages: firstly, they carry well over long distances; and secondly, it is very difficult to locate their source. This latter advantage would have been very important to a *Parasaurolophus* that did not wish its warning signal to make it the center of attention for an approaching attacker.

Beside self-protection, the main purpose of any animal herd is to provide a suitable environment to produce and raise young. Until recently the only real evidence of dinosaur family life were eggs and nests from the Gobi Desert discovered in the 1920s, and some trackways that showed adults and juveniles moving together. Then a spectacular series of discoveries by Dr John Horner in Montana completely transformed our understanding of how certain dinosaurs reared their young, and shed new light on the sophistication of dinosaur social behavior.

The Gobi Desert nests were important because they were the first real evidence that dinosaurs were hatched from eggs. Laid by female *Protoceratops*, the nests consisted of up to twenty elliptical eggs laid upright in layered circles. To achieve this the mother must have first scraped a shallow hole about 3 feet wide and then crouched over it,

DISTINCTIVE HEADS. The different shapes of hadrosaurs' crests might have allowed them to recognize members of their own species and the sex of individuals.

SIGHT AND SOUND. The long crest of this male *Parasaurolophus* acted as a sound and visual signal. Females had a shorter more curved crest so they could be distinguished within the herd.

gradually turning in a tight circle as each new egg was laid. Sand was pushed around the eggs to keep them upright, with the larger end at the top to allow the hatchling to escape. *Protoceratops* was only 6 feet long, but even the largest dinosaur would have laid quite small eggs. Eggs must have a shell thin enough to allow oxygen to pass through the pores in its surface and reach the developing embryo inside, and for the baby inside to break out. Clearly, there was no question of dinosaurs sitting on these fragile objects to incubate them, and *Protoceratops* may have covered her eggs with sand or relied on the surrounding air temperature being high enough to keep the uncovered eggs warm.

NESTING COLONIES

The first indication that some dinosaurs might have nested in colonies came after 1979 when a number of *Orodromeus* nests were found close together on two sites in Montana. Ten years of

painstaking excavation at these sites, and the study of the complete fossil record, has allowed John Horner and his team to build up a much fuller picture of dinosaur nesting behavior.

Both sites were probably small islands off the shore of a shallow lake. Trees grew around the lake and the islands were covered with small plants. Several *Orodromeus* nests were found with eggs

SOUNDING THE ALARM. The 3 feet long skull crest of *Parasaurolophus* housed a complex arrangement of tubes and chambers. Air from the dinosaur's lungs was blown through the tubes (shown in pink) which acted as resonators producing a low note.

laid in clutches of twelve or twenty-four in a spiral arrangement. In this case, however, plant remains around the eggs suggest that *Orodromeus* may have used the incubation technique of piling rotting vegetation, perhaps mixed with sand, on top of the nest and allowing the "compost heap" to keep the eggs warm. Modern scrub fowl do this, removing and adding plants to keep the temperature constant.

A key feature of the *Orodromeus* nests was that the shells of the hatched eggs were found intact except where the top part was split off by the escaping young. This strongly suggests that the young *Orodromeus* walked away from the nest very soon after hatching, possibly under the protection of their mother, just as hens do. A well-developed *Orodromeus* young, found still inside its egg, had fully formed leg bones and joints, and would easily have been able to carry its own weight. The discovery of several half-grown juvenile skeletons suggests that the hatchlings, although mobile, probably stayed near the nesting site for some while.

Minute examination of the areas surrounding the *Orodromeus* nests gave a further insight into the balanced ecological system the dinosaurs were part of, and shows that the nesting colony supported a number of scavengers and predators. There are fossilized skeletons of varanid lizards. Modern varanid lizards frequently prey on the nests of crocodiles

INSIDE THE EGG. Fragments of *Protoceratops* egg show the surface ornament which prevented blockage of the pores, allowing gas exchange through the shell.

and scrub fowl, so their prehistoric ancestors probably invaded the *Orodromeus* nests. Fossil bones of small mammals suggest that they too may have eaten eggs or vulnerable hatchlings on the island. A large number of fossilized insect pupa cases or cocoons were also found. Modern beetles and insects are attracted to nests because the egg fluids and dead young are an easy and rich source of food, so the prehistoric beetles were probably scavenging in the same way. One egg was actually found with the hatchling inside

having been eaten away by insects while still in the shell. Finally, there were discoveries of fossil teeth of the meat-eater *Troodon* and the much larger *Albertosaurus*, both very likely predators on such a choice hunting ground.

HELPLESS HATCHLINGS. *Overleaf:* The *Maiasaura* young were too small and weak to leave the nest after hatching. They remained nest bound for many weeks and were fed and looked after by the adults. This enabled them to grow rapidly but left them vulnerable to attack from predators entering the nesting colony.

CRACKED OPEN. A hatched *Orodromeus* egg; the top third was split off by the hatching young.

One of the most intriguing finds on the island was a number of other dinosaur eggs, quite different from those of *Orodromeus*. These eggs had a bumpy texture and were laid in straight lines, with pairs of eggs lying flat on the ground. A tiny embryo recently discovered shows that they were laid by *Troodon*, placing its own eggs in with the *Orodromeus* eggs to gain protection.

Knowledge of dinosaur nesting habits

took a further leap forward with the discovery, again by John Horner, of another nesting colony in Montana. This one belonged to the plant-eating *Maiasaura* and turned out to have forty nests covering 2.5 acres of ground.

Maiasaura, whose name means "good mother lizard," was a 26 feet long hadrosaur. It built its nesting colonies in dry upland areas, presumably to avoid the danger of flooding and to have a commanding lookout position. This behavior is similar to that of colonial birds such as terns who also rely on the colony to protect them from predators. *Maiasaura* returned to the same nesting site every breeding season and the nests were refurbished and used again. The nests themselves were about 6 feet in diameter in the form of a mud and stone walled basin lined with vegetation. They were spaced one dinosaur length apart so that the parents could come and go without getting in the way of neighbors. Clutches of up to twenty-five eggs were laid in the nests and arranged in circles so that no egg touched another.

Maiasaura used the same method of incubation as *Orodromeus*, piling up plants to form a warm compost layer over the nest. The striking difference between the two dinosaurs is that the *Maiasaura* young stayed in the nest for several weeks being fed by their parents before venturing out into the wider world. We can tell this because of the many fragments of trampled eggshell

found in the nests and the remains of what appears to be regurgitated leaves and berries provided by the parent dinosaurs. The newly hatched *Maiasaura* measured around 12 inches long. Their leg bones and joints were not fully formed and it was not until they reached a length of about 5 feet that they left the nest. This growth would have been quite rapid since staying still and being brought food by your parents is a very effective way to get big quickly (ask any baby starling). By the end of their first year the *Maiasaura* could have reached 8 feet in length and would be ready to migrate with their parents to lowland pastures. How long they stayed together as a family group is not clear. Growth studies of *Maiasaura* using computer modeling estimate that individuals probably reached breeding age at about ten to twelve years. In terms of size, the nearest modern equivalent is a baby elephant which will stay with its mother for fifteen years or more before becoming fully mature and independent.

The nesting behaviors of *Orodromeus* and *Maiasaura* give the clearest indication so far about the social development of dinosaurs. They mirror exactly the two kinds of nesting found among modern birds — "precocial" where babies leave the nest as soon as they hatch, and "altrical" where the helpless young remain in the nest. With *Maiasaura*, the large nesting communities suggest further social development. These dinosaurs must have had some kind of homing instinct, like swallows or pigeons, that guided them back to the same breeding ground year after year. Nest construction must have been instinctive knowledge, but the ability to construct a complex colony in cooperation with others suggests quite high degrees of communication skills. And once the *Maiasaura* young were moving about, the parents must have had some means of recognizing their own babies from among the many others in the breeding colony. Did they do this by smell? By special sounds? By distinguishing marks or colors? These questions are probably unanswerable, but they do show how socially advanced scientists now believe some dinosaurs to have been.

GOOD MOTHER LIZARD. *Above: Maiasaura* herds returned to the same nesting grounds year after year. Nests were built one *Maiasaura* length apart. Up to twenty-five eggs were laid in each nest, and the hatchlings were fed by their parents. *Maiasaura*'s behavior gives an insight into how dinosaurs operated as social animals.

AGILE JUVENILES. *Below:* This nest model is based on finds of *Orodromeus* in Montana. Arranged in a spiral by the mother dinosaur, the clutch of twelve eggs is spaced to allow the hatchlings room to escape. The opened eggs show where the hatchlings have knocked off the tops from within and left the nest immediately.

6 Fossil remains tell us a good deal about dinosaurs' bones and teeth, but much less about the rest of their physical make-up. How did they see and hear? What color were they? Were they warm- or cold-blooded? Skilled research and comparison with modern animals give some insight into the physiology of dinosaurs but many fundamental questions are still unanswered.

T he popular image of dinosaurs is as huge, amazingly shaped creatures more terrifying than the dragons of legend or fairytale. In fact, they were quite ordinary living animals with bodies that had to perform the same basic functions as any dog or turtle or human being. To understand dinosaurs as real live animals we must look beyond the "Did-you-know? Amazing Facts!" about size or weight or length of teeth and examine their biological make-up.

All dinosaurs were built around a bony scaffolding that had the same basic components — skull, spine, ribs, shoulders, hips, legs, and tail. The hips tell us which of the two main groups a dinosaur belongs to. To determine this when looking at a dinosaur skeleton, first find the pelvis or hip girdle, where the back legs join the spine. The pelvis is made up of three bones called the ilium, the ischium, and the pubis. If the ischium and pubis radiate out from the ilium in different directions, with the pubis pointing forward between the legs, then the dinosaur is a saurischian (lizard-hipped). All meat-eating dinosaurs belonged to this group, as did all the plant-eating sauropods and their relatives. Modern lizards and crocodiles have a similar hip structure.

Dinosaurs in the other group have quite different hips, similar superficially to those of modern birds, and hence are called ornithischians (bird-hipped). Here the pubis is swung right back to lie alongside the ischium, pointing backward down the tail. All ornithischians were plant-eaters and they account for the vast majority of dinosaur fossils discovered. Despite their "bird-hipped" group name, however,

there is no evolutionary link between this group of dinosaurs and birds.

BONES AND MUSCLES
Having said that dinosaurs all had the same basic bony scaffolding, the bones themselves show many variations. For the vast plant-eaters, strength was the main requirement and their leg bones were huge and solid, capable of carrying enormous loads. At the same time they developed an ingenious system for reducing the weight of other bones

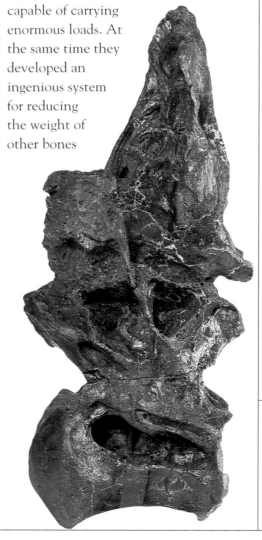

without any loss of strength. The vertebrae of the sauropod *Ornithopsis*, for example, had great hollows, called pleurocoels, scooped out of them. Yet the remaining structure was just as strong as a solid lump of bone despite being nearly 50 percent lighter.

Smaller, fast-moving dinosaurs developed another feature seen in modern animals — thin-walled long bones. In this case the bone is effectively a hollow tube, the thin outer sleeve being made of heavy bone and the center containing much lighter marrow. Such bones give a strong and flexible framework to a modern gazelle with as little extra weight as possible. Fast-running, plant-eating dinosaurs, like *Dryosaurus*, also had hollow long bones, presumably for lightness and therefore extra speed to escape their hunters.

In life, each dinosaur's skeleton was held together by a network of ligaments, muscles, and tendons, just as our bodies are. Some fossil bones actually have "muscle scars" (roughened patches where the muscles were attached) and from these it is possible to work out the size

BONE ENGINEERING. This vertebra from the middle of the backbone of *Ornithopsis*, a large four-legged plant-eater related to *Diplodocus*, has extensive hollows (pleurocoels) to reduce its weight. The bone is virtually a series of struts joined together at critical points to give maximum strength for minimum weight.

(*Previous spread*) STAYING ALIVE. In the late Cretaceous Period in North America three groups of hadrosaurs — *Parasaurolophus*, *Corythosaurus*, and *Lambeosaurus* — sense danger from an approaching predator.

THEM BONES. *Top:* Speed was important to *Dryosaurus*, a small unarmed plant-eater. Thin-walled, hollow bones, similar to the modern gazelle, gave strength without adding weight to the skeleton. *Bottom:* Solid pillarlike limb bones supported the 20–30 ton *Apatosaurus*. This thigh bone is 5 feet long.

and position of some main controlling muscles. A skilled anatomist can further interpret the unique structure of each skeleton to calculate where the muscles were located, how the dinosaur moved, and the overall shape of its body. We also know that, like modern reptiles and birds, dinosaurs had relatively few muscles in their faces and were probably rather expressionless. The fully restored head models you may see in some museums look very similar to dinosaur skulls, being basically just skin over bone with very little extra padding in between.

Yet even here, at this most basic level of building on the bony framework, there is plenty of room for doubt. The legs of a

HIP TALK. The pelvis consists of three bones on each side — ilium (red), ischium (yellow), and pubis (green). *Top:* In saurischian dinosaurs the ischium and pubis point in different directions. *Middle:* Early ornithischians, like *Scelidosaurus,* have the ischium and pubis lying together and pointing backward toward the tail. *Bottom:* Later ornithischians, like *Iguanodon,* developed an extra forward-facing prong on the pubis. This does not make them saurischians.

MUSCLE POWER. Dinosaurs' muscles gave them both strength and dexterity. *Top:* Huge sheets of muscle kept the heavy skeleton of *Brachiosaurus* together and allowed it to move. *Bottom: Iguanodon's* arm was controlled by a complex muscle system.

large plant-eater like *Diplodocus*, for example, must have been moved by huge sheets and bunches of muscle of which there is no trace in the fossilized remains. The expanding jaws of *Tyrannosaurus* were controlled by a set of muscles and tendons that interacted with each other in highly complex ways. How far could *Tenontosaurus* move its tail up and down, and how far from side to side? Did *Albertosaurus* have a deep muscular throat like a bulldog or a high ridge of muscle at the back of its neck? No one knowns for certain and, while modern animals can sometimes provide clues, this is certainly not hard evidence.

Fundamentally, the amount and relative proportions of muscle that you think each dinosaur carried is linked with how you believe it moved and lived. It is fascinating to see the different illustrations of the same dinosaur over the years as views have changed about its way of life. Early pictures of *Tyrannosaurus*, for example, show it draped in quite puny muscles consistent with the sluggish animal it was thought to be. More recent ideas of *Tyrannosaurus* as an active hunter have produced illustrations which show a huge, muscular animal. One of the joys, and also the hazards, of dinosaur study is how much is left open to interpretation.

BONE SCARS. The rough patches (as shaded) on this *Iguanodon* metatarsal (long bone of foot) show where the muscles and tendons were attached.

SKIN AND ARMOR

Over the top of their skeleton and supporting muscles, each dinosaur wore a skin and a variety of scales, plates, spines, claws, and horns. As described in Chapter 4 (Attack and Defense), fossilized skin is very rare but we know that it is made up of thousands of small bony plates (called osteoderms) embedded in the skin, rather like the covering of an alligator or a lizard.

On the heavily armored ankylosaurs the bigger plates and scales formed a defensive barrier to prevent attack. On *Stegosaurus*, the large chevron-shaped back plates are no longer thought to be primarily for defense (they would have been useless for protecting the most vulnerable belly parts in any case) but rather to be part of a body heating and cooling system. *Stegosaurus* pumped blood up through the skin that covered the plates and, by standing side on to the Sun, could use them for rapid warming. If it was too hot, it simply had to move into the shade or face the Sun so that the minimum plate area was exposed. A similar feature has been found in a little-known group of theropod dinosaurs called spinosaurids and in a relative of *Iguanodon* called *Ouranosaurus*. These dinosaurs had elongated back spines up to 6 feet long which may have supported a huge saillike fin. Such fins would have provided an enormous surface area for heating or cooling blood.

Claws and horns were supported by a bony core and sheathed in a covering of tough keratin, the same substance that your fingernails are made of. Claw and horn cores have a groove running along one or both sides that was used to anchor the horn covering. Plant-eaters' claws were usually blunt or hooflike but meat-eaters' claws were sharply pointed.

We have looked already at dinosaur coloring but it is worth repeating here that any ideas about the color of dinosaurs' skin is speculation rather than fact. Even more controversial is the question of whether some dinosaurs had feathers. This remarkable idea was first suggested in the late 1970s by the Russian scientist S. M. Kurzanov when studying the small meat-eating *Avimimus*. He thought that the upper arm bones of this dinosaur showed feather attachment points similar to those that can be seen in modern birds. If *Avimimus* had this feature, Kurzanov reasoned, other related meat-eaters probably had it too. The evidence is disputed but has been taken up enthusiastically by a number of dinosaur experts and illustrators.

Why feathers? It is generally agreed that birds evolved from small meat-eating theropod dinosaurs. Obviously these

SHARP ENCOUNTERS. The strong horny covering of *Triceratops'* bony horn cores made them fearsome weapons. Even a large hunter like *Tyrannosaurus* could easily sustain a fatal injury from a single thrust.

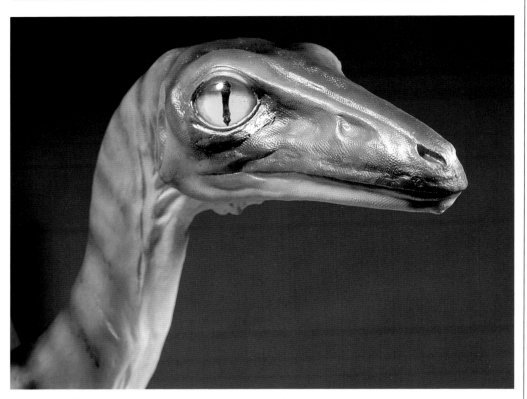

BRIGHT EYES. The large eyes and brain of *Troodon* suggest it was intelligent and active.

percentage of the cavity occupied by the brain (not all the space was actually filled with brain), this will give you the actual brain size.

There is no doubt that some dinosaurs got by with very little by way of brain. *Stegosaurus*, for example, weighed 3.2 tons and had just 2 ounces of brain, thirty times less than an elephant of the same weight. The ratio of brain to body weight in the large sauropods is even more dramatic, 100,000:1. Yet this is hardly surprising. Everything we know about these dinosaurs suggests that they led lives that demanded little brain work. *Brachiosaurus* did not have to hunt its food or evade predators, both activities that need brain power. *Stegosaurus* may well have lived in herds or family groups, but was not crucially dependent for survival on herd communication and rapid reaction, as were the unarmored (and therefore far more intelligent) hadrosaurs. Simple lives demand less control and coordination.

What we should expect to find is increasing brain size and complexity in line with the demands made by the dinosaurs' lifestyle — slow plant-eaters at the bottom, herders and pack hunters in the middle, and fast-running stalker hunters at the top. This is actually what Professor James Hopson of the University of Chicago, discovered when he compared dinosaur brain and body sizes to determine the "braininess" of different groups. According to his research the "league table" of intelligence runs, from the bottom up: sauropods, ankylosaurs, stegosaurs, ceratopians, ornithopods, carnosaurs, and coelurosaurs.

dinosaurs did not sprout feathers overnight and become birds, so there must have been a long period when some of the small theropods were experimenting with feathers, which are only a different version of scales. Feathers would have been useful not for flight but for insulation and display, so perhaps some small meat-eaters kept them right to the end of the dinosaur era. It is quite legitimate, say the feather enthusiasts, to illustrate such dinosaurs with downy feathers, neck plumage, arm, and even tail feathers. The US artist Gregory Paul draws all his small theropods with feathers as a matter of principle, ranging from fluffy baby *Velociraptor* to adults with virtual Indian Chief headdresses. Such ideas may not be generally accepted, but they show how far some dinosaur experts are prepared to go in stressing the direct link between dinosaurs and birds.

CLEVER OR DUMB?

Were dinosaurs stupid? Describing *Brontosaurus* (now called *Apatosaurus*) in 1883, the great US paleontologist Othniel Marsh stated that its tiny brain proved it to be a "stupid, slow moving reptile," words which probably still sum up the general view of all dinosaurs' mental abilities. The facts tell a rather different story, as we can see when we start to look in detail at the dinosaurs' senses and the brains that controlled them.

Much work has been undertaken recently to determine the size of dinosaurs' brains relative to their body weight. This is fairly easy to do where there is a well-preserved skull, since all dinosaurs had brains enclosed in a tough bony case. If you measure the volume of this braincase inside the skull and take into account the variation in the

The structure of dinosaur skulls also provides clues to the relative size, importance, and complexity of their sense organs, and hence their brains. For example, large forward-pointing eye-sockets suggest a sight-dominant animal; large spaces in the snout could mean the sense of smell was important.

Most dinosaurs had monocular vision with eyes set at the sides of their heads, and very little overlap between the left and right fields of view. This gave them a good wide-angled view of their surroundings but no real ability to judge distances. For this, front-facing eyes are required and considerable brain power to process and interpret the visual information. There is evidence that some of the big meat-eaters like *Tyrannosaurus* had at least some binocular overlap, but the dinosaurs which developed fully binocular vision were the smaller meat-eaters. Their brains were particularly well developed in the area that controlled the co-ordination between running, hand movement, and visual information about moving objects. This was the key to the hunting success of dinosaurs like *Troodon* that stalked and chased scuttling mammals and lizards. It had exceptionally large eyes, based on the size of the eye sockets, and the biggest brain of any dinosaur relative to its body size — certainly up to the level of some modern birds and mammals.

Just how dinosaurs saw the world we will never know. Some reptiles see in color, as do most birds, which have the keenest of vision of all living animals. Hawks, for example, have up to eight times more visual cells packed into the most sensitive spot of their eyes than we do,

BRAIN BOX. In this *Iguanodon* braincase, the brain tissue decayed before fossilization, leaving a hollow space. A silicone rubber cast shows the approximate shape of the brain as it would have fitted in the braincase.

allowing them to recognize shapes that would only be blurs to us. The relative size of birds' eyeballs is also huge, in some cases taking up more space than the brain itself (an ostrich's eye is the size of a tennis ball). All the evidence suggests that sight was also a critical sense for the dinosaurs, ranging from the limited low-level view of *Protoceratops* or *Tuojiangosaurus*, through the wide-angled horizon-scanning lookout ability of the hadrosaurs or iguanodontids, up to the keen hunter's vision of *Troodon*.

Dinosaurs did not have exterior ear flaps like mammals, but heard through holes set far back in the head behind their

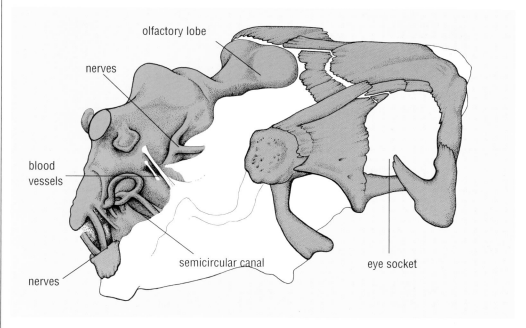

TASTE, SMELL, BALANCE. Drawing of part of an *Iguanodon* skull (purple) from an original fossil showing a preserved brain (orange, the equivalent of the silicone cast in the figure above) prepared from the surrounding rock (white). The large olfactory lobe at the front suggests it had a well-developed sense of smell. Nerves and blood vessels to the eyes, face and ears can be seen. Even the semicircular canal inside the ear is preserved. This would have given *Iguanodon* its sense of balance.

eyes. Today's reptiles and birds have a similar arrangement with a slitlike external ear opening leading to the hearing organs in the brain. For birds in particular, hearing is an important part of their social behavior, closely linked with their ability to communicate by song. A male bird can have several hundred songs in its repertoire, each with a particular meaning understood by other members of the same species. It was probably herding dinosaurs, with their strong need to communicate, that had the most acute sense of hearing. Indeed, hadrosaurs display the only real evidence so far discovered of being able to make noises, with a variety

OLD AGE. Very few animals die of old age in the wild. Disease, predators, accident, or injury are more likely causes of death. The fossil evidence suggests that dinosaurs were the same. Although there is no direct evidence, best estimates put the life expectancy of large dinosaurs within the range of today's longest lived animals, 70–130 years.

Left: An *Iguanodon* foot showing hard frills of arthritic growth on the toe joints.
Opposite: This *Iguanodon* hip bone was fractured during its life and healed slightly out of alignment.

of nasal trumpets and air sacs. Such equipment could not produce the complex trills, tiny pauses, and extra-high notes achieved by birds, but they could certainly have allowed the development of a basic hadrosaur language for warning and directing the herd, as well as playing a crucial role at mating time. Cooperative hunters like *Deinonychus* would also have needed to communicate when stalking or bringing down a victim. Judging by the behavior of modern pack animals, however, this was probably a much more visual than noise-based language (lying in ambush or running at full pelt are hardly ideal moments to bark orders).

Dinosaurs, like many modern land animals, would probably have made noises as and when the occasion demanded — to defend territory, attract a mate, see off an enemy, or warn of danger. If we were able to play back a "sound track" of the dinosaur era, we would probably hear a good range of snuffles, squeaks, grunts, chirps, snarls, roars, and howls.

The senses of taste and smell are closely linked in all animals, being controlled by the same part of the brain. They are

used by hunters and hunted to keep track of each other, by some plant-eaters to discriminate between attractive and unsuitable food, and, in many species, as part of the mating process. It is hard to believe that the big meat-eaters like *Allosaurus* did much tasting of the meat they bolted down their huge throats. Their tongues were probably simple and rough, designed to position chunks of meat for swallowing as fast as possible. Plant-eaters, particularly those that chewed their food, would have needed more mobile tongues to move the wads of vegetation to the correct position for chopping and grinding. One of the very rare fossil brains that has been preserved, that of an *Iguanodon*, shows well-developed olfactory lobes (the section of the brain dealing with smell and taste) at the front of the brain. *Iguanodon* certainly had a large, broad snout to accommodate nostrils and sense organs, so perhaps this dinosaur at least had a keen sense of smell and relished the taste of its food.

The sense of touch cannot have been very well developed in any dinosaur, simply because of the nature of their skin. Bony plates embedded in a thick hide are not designed for sensitivity and dinosaurs could have scraped and blundered their way past trees and rocks without feeling very much at all. Alligators have sensitive skin spots on their snouts and necks which they rub against each other at mating times. Is it too fanciful to see a pair of *Tyrannosaurus* doing the same? Or a couple of *Diplodocus* with necks lovingly entwined having a quick nuzzle in the high branches?

Looking at dinosaur senses does not produce a definitive answer as to whether they were clever or stupid. Indeed, these terms are not really relevant since they imply that dinosaurs would have somehow been "better off" if they had more humanlike intelligence. The fact is that each species of dinosaur had all the brain power it needed to succeed at its own way of life for many millions of years. If humans achieve a fraction of this, we shall be doing well.

THE BLOOD QUESTION

Were dinosaurs warm- or cold-blooded? Dinosaur experts care passionately about this subject, many of them holding radically opposed and irreconcilable views. To understand why this debate has raged so fiercely for the last twenty years we must start by looking at the nature of warm- and cold-bloodedness itself.

Animals function most efficiently if their body temperature is fairly constant. The chemical reactions that take place in a body work best at set temperatures and if these go up or down too far, the body ceases to operate properly. So-called cold-blooded animals, like lizards and snakes, control their body temperature by their behavior, moving in and out of the Sun during the day. This is called the ectothermic ("outside heat") method. Warm-blooded animals (birds and mammals) convert food energy into body heat, the endothermic ("inside heat")

method. To cool off, endothermic animals sweat, pant, wallow in water, or, in the case of an elephant, flap their ears to cool down the blood that flows through them.

There are advantages and disadvantages to both systems. A warm-blooded dog burns off its food energy very rapidly and needs to eat nearly ten times more than a cold-blooded lizard of the same size. On the other hand, a lizard must spend several hours a day basking in the Sun to warm up and cannot operate effectively at night or when the surrounding temperature drops. More importantly, as far as the dinosaurs are concerned, warm-blooded animals can support much larger brains and more active lifestyles than cold-blooded ones because brains in particular need constant temperatures to function efficiently. So the issue of warm or cold blood actually determines the whole way you look at dinosaurs — sluggish and dim, or active and intelligent more like today's mammals and birds. No wonder dinosaur experts think it is so

LARGE AND SMALL. Dinosaurs had very varied lifestyles ranging from huge slow-moving plant-eaters to smaller, active hunters. Did they also have a range of different warm- and cold-blooded metabolisms?

important. The evidence quoted by each side can be complex and controversial but the main issues are easy to understand.

Many of the big dinosaurs held their heads high above their bodies — *Tyrannosaurus* and *Iguanodon* are examples and *Brachiosaurus* an extreme case. To pump blood up to their brains would have required high pressure, far higher than the delicate blood vessels in their lungs could withstand. Warm-blooded birds and mammals deal with this problem by having two blood circuits — a low-pressure one to pick up oxygen and release carbon dioxide in the lungs, and a high-pressure one to transport oxygen and nutrients to the rest of the body. Their hearts are internally divided and run the two circuits side by side. Lofty dinosaurs would also have needed a divided heart and, say some scientists, this suggests their bodies worked like those of warm-blooded birds and mammals. It is this final link in the logic that is controversial. Some dinosaurs must indeed have had a divided heart, or something very like it, to get the blood

NEAR THE BONE. Haversian bone has many blood vessels with dense bony rings around them. Today's large warm-blooded mammals have this type of bone. This section is from the rib of a horse.

Some dinosaurs also had Haversian bone. This section of a *Baryonyx* rib shows the same bony ring structure as the horse. Does this mean that dinosaurs with Haversian bone were warm-blooded?

Dinosaurs, birds and mammals all have similar primary bone with many blood vessels. This type of bone, called fibro-lamellar bone (shown here from a sauropod limb bone), is the first to be formed during rapid growth.

Modern cold-blooded reptiles show growth rings in their bones indicating that they grow at different rates. But some dinosaurs, as in this iguanodont limb bone, also show this feature.

So dinosaurs had all three kinds of bone, evidence of a physiology in between that of cold-blooded reptiles and warm-blooded mammals and birds.

to their heads, but they would not necessarily need to be fully warm-blooded to achieve this. Modern alligators have a functionally divided heart and remain cold-blooded. There is a great energy saving advantage in using the Sun to warm up rather than having to go and find food to do the same job. In evolutionary terms, dinosaurs may have retained this advantage as long as possible, perhaps combining a version of the warm-blooded heart and lung system with cold-blooded ways to control body temperature.

The huge size of some dinosaurs and active lifestyles of others have also been put forward as arguments for warm-bloodedness. A 30 ton sauropod could never warm up in the Sun, it is said, because its surface area was so small compared to its volume. At the other end of the scale, a fast-running, leaping, back-claw slasher like *Deinonychus* could never have maintained such a high level of activity without having a warm-blooded animal's ability to generate its own body heat.

Yet these arguments may seem less convincing when you remember the unchanging warm climate that persisted during most of the dinosaur era. Under these conditions, the large body and small surface area of a huge plant-eater like *Diplodocus* would have prevented it cooling down, enabling it to maintain a constant body temperature. Indeed, with the heat generated by its fermenting tank stomach, the problem might well have been how to lose heat rather than keep it. As for *Deinonychus*, just because it could run and jump does not mean it did so very often. As a cold-blooded hunter it could afford to kill and eat far

less often than if it were warm-blooded, leaving plenty of time to top up body heat levels by sun-basking. The most we can say is that, on balance, the intelligent pack-hunter's life led by *Deinonychus* points strongly toward it having a physiology similar to modern birds and mammals.

Microscopic study of thin sections of dinosaur bone has provided more clues, and controversy, about dinosaur physiology. Some dinosaur bone shows the same kind of microscopic structure as that of large modern mammals, which contains many blood vessels. This kind of bone (Haversian bone) is formed by "remodeling" the bone tissues as the animal grows to provide more stress resistance and strength. It is accomplished by laying down dense tubes of bony tissue round each of the many blood vessels. Since dinosaurs had the same kind of bone this could mean that they were warm-blooded like mammals, say the hot-blooded dinosaur supporters. However, detailed studies on many different dinosaurs, particularly by Dr Robin Reid, at the Queen's University of Belfast, Northern Ireland, have shown that the evidence is just not that simple.

In many dinosaurs, the bone formed first during rapid growth (the primary bone) is similar to that of birds and mammals with blood vessels. This is an important difference between dinosaurs and modern reptiles that lay down their bone in seasonal growth rings a little like tree rings. However, some dinosaurs show this kind of bone too and up to a point it can give some idea of the age of an individual, except that we do not know if one ring equals one year! So,

dinosaurs have three types of bony tissue: primary bone, Haversian bone, and growth ring bone, and it varies between bones and even within the same bone.

What does all this mean? The work of Dr Reid and others has shown that dinosaurs could grow very rapidly (as fast as birds and mammals) when they were young as they had a lot of primary bone tissue, especially in their legs. This tissue was sometimes replaced by secondary (Haversian) bone to give strength and stress resistance as it does in large mammals today. The seasonal growth rings support the idea that their growth slowed down later in life and became more reptilelike. As Dr Reid suggests, dinosaurs were not quite like reptiles, birds, or mammals, but had a uniquely dinosaurian physiology all of their own.

There is plenty more to be said on this subject and volumes of detailed study to read. What it all amounts to is a definite "maybe" about dinosaur warm- and cold-bloodedness. Yet this does not negate what we do know, which is plenty, about how dinosaurs looked and lived. *Brachiosaurus* was really huge, *Deinonychus* did sprint and leap on to its victims, *Tyrannosaurus* was the largest meat-eater ever to live on Earth. How they managed to do these things may be debatable, but the fact is that they did them as real eating, breathing, sleeping, running, living animals.

WHERE DID

7 Some catastrophic event wiped out the dinosaurs. Was it an asteroid collision? Or a climate change brought about by massive volcanic eruptions? Buried under tons of rock,

THEY GO?

the evidence is elusive and controversial. Yet it all points to the dinosaurs' involvement in one of the most disastrous mass-extinctions in the Earth's history.

Why do animals die out? Every species evolves to exploit a particular environment, sometimes in a very specialized way. The koala bear, for example, is the only mammal that can survive on a diet of eucalyptus leaves, thanks to a unique digestive system and an extraordinarily long gut. While this diet means it is restricted to living in eucalyptus-growing areas, there is no competition for its food supply. The koala bears can have their eucalyptus trees to themselves, eating just 2 pounds of leaves each night and sleeping for twenty-two hours out of twenty-four.

On the other hand, beetles have adapted to thrive almost anywhere. By virtually any measurement they are one of today's most successful animal groups with at least half a million species so far described, distributed over virtually every part of the Earth's surface. Indeed, if beetles were allowed to develop unchecked for just a few months, the whole land surface of the planet would be covered with them. While beetles and koala bears have evolved quite differently, they both owe their success to the same cause — being adapted to do better in a particular part of the ecosystem than any other animal. Being well adapted to an environment is all very well, except for one thing — the environment itself is constantly changing. Extinction can happen when a species does not adapt quickly enough to meet these changes.

For over 160 million years dinosaurs were champion adapters. Although each individual species may only have survived for 2–3 million years, the dinosaur group as a whole was remarkably good at meeting any new conditions. As explained in Chapter 1, continents moved, sea levels rose and fell, volcanoes erupted, weather patterns changed, and new plants appeared, but the dinosaurs thrived on it all. They were diverse, they lived on every continent, and they totally dominated the land. Then, quite suddenly, they all disappeared. What happened? Almost everyone now accepts that dinosaurs were wiped out by a sudden, catastrophic event or events that affected the Earth's climate. This change was so dramatic and so fast that the dinosaurs had no chance to adapt before the new conditions killed them. What no one can say for certain is how the event came about.

THE END OF THE DINOSAUR ERA

This is what we do know. During the last few million years of the dinosaur era, a more seasonal climatic pattern of warm summers and cool winters developed, particularly at high latitudes. This was influenced by changes in the seas and oceans as the continents moved apart. The fossil record shows that in western North America, which has produced the only extensive latest Cretaceous dinosaur fauna, a small number of very successful plant-eaters dominated the scene. These included a hadrosaur, *Edmontosaurus*, and a ceratopian, *Triceratops*. Meat-eaters like *Tyrannosaurus* and *Troodon* hunted and scavenged on the fringes of the herds.

It now seems possible that the herds themselves migrated over much larger distances than scientists originally thought. Abundant remains of *Edmontosaurus*, together with bones of a horned dinosaur, *Pachyrhinosaurus*, and teeth of a large tyrannosaurid have been found on the North Slope of Alaska, which was well inside the Arctic Circle even 70–65 million years ago. This discovery, made in 1986, indicates that dinosaurs could live at high latitudes even though the climate was cool and there was a long period of darkness in winter (but no polar ice-caps as there are today). The associated plant remains tell us that the temperature ranged from an average 50–53°F in the warmest month down to 35–39°F during the coldest. Did the dinosaurs live there all year round, spending three months in cold, dark conditions? It seems very unlikely. A much more plausible explanation is that herds of plant-eaters, followed by their predators, migrated northward through western Canada in spring in search of fresh food supplies. Modern caribou do just the same today.

Finally, the fossil record shows that dinosaurs were only some of the victims of the dramatic events 65 million years ago. Other animal groups were drastically

(*Previous spread*) PRESERVED IN ROCK. The skeleton of an *Edmontosaurus*, one of the last dinosaurs, lies half-buried in rock exactly as it died.

BECOMING EXTINCT. Rapid environmental changes can push species to extinction as conditions alter faster than the animals can adapt to meet them. *Bottom left:* The Pilori muskrat lived on the island of Martinique. The whole species was wiped out in 1902 when the eruption of Mount Pelée destroyed its habitat. *Bottom right:* The Irish giant deer was once found across Europe. The last survivors in Ireland died when a mini ice age destroyed their food supply. As with the dodo on Mauritius *(top)*, exterminated by sailors hunting it for food, human beings are responsible for most of today's extinctions, polluting and destroying natural habitats. The environmental catastrophe that overtook the dinosaurs was on a more global scale.

reduced or disappeared. In the seas, all the plesiosaurs and mosasaurs vanished and the only group of marine reptiles to survive were turtles. Ammonites and belemnites (relatives of octopus and squid) were wiped out completely, together with most chalky plankton, brachiopods, and clams. In the air, the pterosaurs disappeared but the birds did not. On land the mammals survived as did all other reptile groups (crocodiles, lizards, snakes, tortoises, and turtles) as well as amphibians, insects, and other invertebrates. Extinctions varied among major groups of plants, being most drastic among flowering plants, less so among conifers and least among ferns and mosses.

So much for the facts. Beyond this point everything is based on evidence that is incomplete and impossible to confirm. It is rather like investigating a murder committed 65 million years ago with no surviving witnesses and most of the scene of the crime under several layers of rock. The rest of this chapter takes a look at some of the most likely theories.

INTERPRETING THE EVIDENCE

As mentioned earlier, there is only one area in the world where the end of the dinosaur era can be extensively studied — the western interior of North America where the late Cretaceous and early Tertiary fossil record is most complete and the rocks are best exposed. New collecting techniques in this area have led to some surprising interpretations of the dinosaurs' disappearance.

In the past, paleontologists had always looked for new or relatively complete fossil skeletons to excavate. Many other smaller pieces of fossil bone on the same site were ignored or left in the ground. The emphasis was on the quality of the specimens rather than the quantity. Yet these fossil "leftovers" reveal important information as well. In particular, they can form the basis for estimating the number and type of dinosaurs that inhabited an area at one time. Collecting and identifying these fossil bones is rather like taking a population census — there is a margin of error in the data, but overall patterns and changes through time can be seen.

Over the last few years, US paleontologists have undertaken systematic fossil quantity analysis of rocks from the very end of the Cretaceous Period in the Hell Creek area of northwest Montana, using measurements like the number of teeth per ton of rock or the number of different species per cubic yard. The results show that, in this area at least,

dinosaur diversity (the number of different species) was in decline at the end of the Cretaceous, while mammals were increasing in number, variety, and size to fill the gap. In other words, the dinosaurs were dying out for the whole of their last 5 million years or so and did not simply disappear suddenly.

One reason could be that the climate changes during this period may have broken up the dinosaurs' usual feeding grounds into smaller isolated areas. Conditions generally became wetter, with swamps and rivers fragmenting what had once been huge ranges. The large herds of plant-eaters could have found it increasingly difficult to survive, cut off from each other and having to compete for smaller areas of territory. Since plant-eaters were the base of the dinosaur food chain, their decline would have directly impacted all the hunters and scavengers as well. In this hypothesis we see the dinosaur communities becoming isolated in small pockets of land and dying out one by one. Mammals began to take over the vacant space, but did not develop to their later levels of variety and number until some time after the last dinosaur had gone.

The dinosaur extinction comes at a point in the Earth's history when the Cretaceous rocks were being overlaid by the distinctive Tertiary rocks. This point is called the K–T boundary (K from the Greek word for chalk, *kreta*, after the great thickness of chalk rocks laid down in the sea by chalk plankton during the

BLASTED ROCK. Distinctive parallel lines running across this "shocked" quartz crystal show it has been formed during violent conditions of enormous temperature and pressure, such as a meteorite impact or a nuclear explosion. Similar crystals are found in K–T boundary rocks.

ASTEROID SIGNATURE. A pencil thin layer of clay marks the boundary between Cretaceous and Tertiary rocks. Its high iridium content can only have come from one of two places — a massive volcanic eruption from the Earth's molten interior or an asteroid strike from space. Either would have meant disaster for the dinosaurs.

Cretaceous). It has been close examination of K–T boundary rocks around the world that has given rise to many new ideas about the mass extinction that included the dinosaurs.

THE ASTEROID THEORY

In 1978 Luis and Walter Alvarez, with a team from the University of California at Berkeley, were studying the K–T boundary rocks at Gubbio in Italy. A layer of red clay about 0.75 inch thick just at the boundary point attracted their attention. Tests showed that it contained a level of the element iridium over thirty times higher than the average. Iridium is a very rare element in the Earth's crust. It usually arrives in the cosmic dust from space that is constantly showering the planet or, more unusually, from the Earth's core when certain types of volcano erupt. The high level "iridium spike" led them to suggest that a huge asteroid, up to 6 miles across, must have hit the Earth 65 million years ago, leaving its iridium "signature" in the rocks of the K–T boundary.

Such an event would certainly have been devastating for the dinosaurs. As

DEATH FROM OUTER SPACE? A fireball passing through the Earth's atmosphere leaves a trail of increasing brilliance and explodes just beyond the field of view, South Galactic Pole, September 1991. Such a meteorite hitting the Earth may have resulted in: a primary blast wave equal to thousands of nuclear bombs; a chain reaction of volcanic eruptions; dust and gases filling the atmosphere blocking out the Sun for months and causing acid rain; tidal waves sweeping back and forth against the coasts.

FERN INVASION. K–T boundary fossils show that a short-term fern takeover followed the dinosaur extinction. Similar "fern spikes" occur after volcanoes erupt today, and indicate a major change to the environment.

the asteroid struck at 60,000 mph a primary blast wave would have destroyed everything within a 250–300 mile radius. The same impact would also have sent tidal waves crashing against all the continents and set up a chain reaction of volcanic eruptions. The asteroid itself would probably have vaporized, sending up a huge cloud of dust, gases, and water vapor into the atmosphere. The dust would gradually spread and cause a global winter of darkness lasting up to three months. The asteroid would also cause heating of the atmosphere, leading to chemical reactions producing acid gases such as nitrous oxide that would have washed out as acid rain.

Under these conditions no large animal, and no dinosaur large or small, could have survived. The land creatures best able to live through such an environmental disaster would be small active scavengers, able to find their food from a range of sources — mammals and birds, in fact. In the sea the plankton

would die and the food chain that supported the large marine reptiles would collapse. The disturbance caused to shallow continental shelves as seawater, low in oxygen, was churned up from the deep sea, or acid rain fell, could account for the disappearance of the shelled sea animals — from plankton to ammonites.

Since the sensational publication of these ideas in 1979 (quickly dubbed the "Worst Weekend in the History of the World"), other investigations of the K–T boundary have revealed further information. Most importantly, the "iridium spike" that the Alvarez' discovered at Gubbio has been found at over fifty other places around the world, confirming beyond doubt that some extraordinary event occurred at this time. Microscopic examination of the sediments has also shown the presence of tiny grains of glass (quartz) with criss-cross fractures running across them. "Shocked quartz," as it is called, is also

found at the sites of nuclear explosions and its presence at the K–T boundary suggests there could indeed have been an explosive impact.

The plant fossils at the K–T boundary also show evidence of short-term dramatic change. Just above the boundary, that is just after the event, there is a big increase in the number of fern spores found in the sediments. This has been seen as a rapid recolonization by the wind-dispersed ferns of the devastated mid-continental regions. The trees and shrubs were soon back in force, however, although not necessarily the same ones that were most abundant at the time of the catastrophe. Rare species, and species that were previously found in quite different areas, were the ones that seem to finally dominate the post-dinosaur landscape. This is very similar to what happens when a volcano erupts today, severely cutting back the surrounding plants and allowing the hardy ferns to dominate. After a short while the other plants grow back from buried seeds and rootstock, or seeds transported in from other areas, to regain their former balance. Again the K–T boundary gives us enough information to speculate but not enough to draw firm conclusions.

If an asteroid did hit the Earth, where did it land? Estimates put the crater size at 110 miles across, but when the Alvarez' theory was published no positive sign of it had been found, even using satellite photography. This led to suggestions that the impact point was on part of the seabed that has since disappeared, but in 1990 the remains of an impact crater were found on the seabed off the northwest tip of the

LANDING SITE? *Above:* This crater, 0.75 mile wide and 560 feet deep, in Arizona was made by a small meteor. A hole 110 mile wide would have been punched in the Earth's surface by the K–T boundary asteroid. *Below:* Recent research suggests the asteroid may have landed in the sea just off the tip of the Yucatan Peninsula.

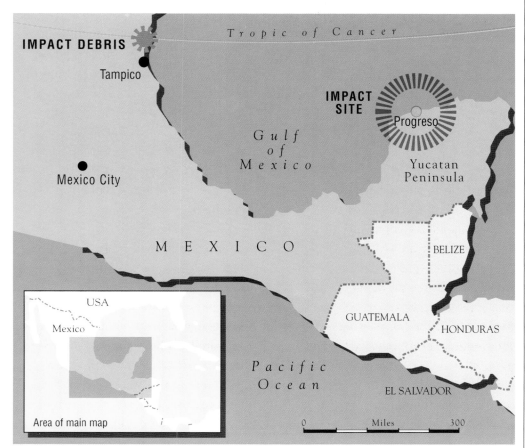

Yucatan Peninsula in Mexico. Possible debris from the explosion (shocked quartz and fossil tree remains mixed up with ocean bedrock) have been found up to 500 miles away, indicating the terrific power of the initial explosion.

THE VOLCANIC THEORY

Sampling of rocks above and below the K–T boundary have shown that the "iridium spike" discovered by the Alvarez' was only one of several, separated by as much as half a million years. It is most unlikely that the Earth was struck by a succession of asteroids over this period, and so some scientists believe we should look to the other source of iridium for an explanation — the Earth's core.

These scientists argue that sustained volcanic eruption would have been enough to bring about the climate change that caused the dinosaur extinction. The effects on the environment of massive volcanic activity would have been quite similar to those of an asteroid impact. There certainly were huge volcanic eruptions in the Deccan Region of India around 66 million years ago that went on discontinuously for a million years and produced flood basalt lava flows which now form the Deccan Traps — layers of rock up to 7900 feet thick. It is equally likely that these eruptions pushed the iridium rich lava to the surface and at the same time pumped huge amounts of carbon dioxide into the atmosphere, which ultimately led to acidification of the seas and the collapse of the marine ecosystem, and altered weather patterns. This pushed the dinosaurs beyond their capacity to adapt and survive.

DEATH FROM THE EARTH'S CORE? *Left:* Could volcanic activity 65 million years ago have altered the global environment, causing the death of the dinosaurs? *Above:* Deposits of cooled lava that form the Deccan Traps in India show that massive volcanic eruptions did occur around this time.

Volcanic activity may have affected dinosaurs in a quite different way as well — by destroying their eggs in the nest. Obviously the egg stage was the point in their life cycle at which dinosaurs were at their most vulnerable, a good reason for looking at their eggs as the possible "weak link" that led to extinction.

The idea that eggs could be affected by volcanic activity is based on the fact that one of the rare elements released from deep inside the Earth by the Deccan Traps volcanism was selenium. Traces have been detected in K–T boundary sediments as far away as Denmark, and unexpectedly high levels were found in the eggshells from nests of sauropod dinosaurs from the latest Cretaceous in France. The amount of selenium in the shells increased in the eggs closest to the K–T boundary and these nests appear to have had a higher rate of hatching failure. Selenium is very poisonous, especially to growing embryos, and very small amounts in hen eggs causes them to die. Dr Hans Hansen, of the University of Copenhagen, Denmark, who carried out this work, has suggested that plant-eating dinosaurs suffered strongly reduced hatching as a result of eating large quantities of vegetation covered with volcanic dust containing selenium. This reproductive decline could in time have led to a complete breakdown of the food chain.

DEATH IN THE NEST

Another, now discredited, egg theory was that some small mammals developed the ability to crack open and eat dinosaur eggs, rather as a mongoose does with bird and reptile eggs today. Whole dinosaur generations would thus be wiped out before they even left the nest. Attractive though it might appear, this idea simply does not stand up to detailed study. It is possible that some mammals, and even some dinosaurs, were egg eaters. *Oviraptor*, for example, had a powerful jaw that could have cracked eggs, and a *Velociraptor* skeleton has been found just above a nest of *Protoceratops* eggs. Yet modern egg eaters never actually destroy the species they feed off, since this would endanger their own food supply. It is not credible that the Cretaceous mammals would have disobeyed such a basic rule of scavenger survival.

A more intriguing egg-based explanation for dinosaur extinction relates to egg temperature. In crocodiles, alligators, and some lizards and turtles the temperature of their eggs during incubation determines whether the hatchling will be male or female. For example, American alligator eggs incubated at less than 86°F produce all females, at 90°F produce males and females, and at 93°F all males. If some dinosaurs had the same mechanism, and if the climate changes included an overall rise or fall in temperature of just a few degrees, then it is possible that the dinosaurs started to produce far more of one sex than the other, unbalancing the population to the point of extinction.

So what really happened? No one knows for certain. There is clear evidence that the Earth's climate was changing toward the end of the Cretaceous Period. Also that two catastrophic events occurred — the sudden asteroid impact (in Mexico) and the longer term Deccan Traps volcanic activity. It may well be that the combined effects of all three events, in varying proportions in different parts of the world, proved to be too traumatic for the dinosaurs.

What we do know is that any theory which explains the disappearance of the dinosaurs alone is only telling us half the story (this is the real weakness of the egg theories). The extinction at the end of the Cretaceous shows puzzling patterns that neither a single big explosion nor a long drawn out decline can fully account for. What event, or combination of events, would prove equally fatal to a huge meat-eater like *Tyrannosaurus*, a medium sized plant-eater like *Edmontosaurus*, and a fast-running hunter like *Troodon*? What event would kill all dinosaurs and yet leave crocodiles unaffected? What event would kill flying reptiles like pterosaurs but not birds? What event would hit so many marine animals but miss sea turtles and reef corals? The only common pattern seems to be that it was fatal to be big. With very rare exceptions, anything over

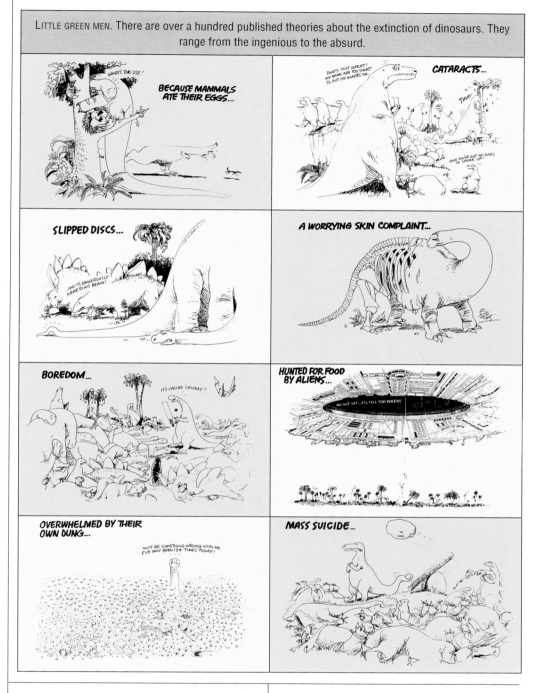

LITTLE GREEN MEN. There are over a hundred published theories about the extinction of dinosaurs. They range from the ingenious to the absurd.

3 feet long or 65 pounds in weight on land, air, or sea fell victim to the Cretaceous mass extinction.

As we undertake more detective work to unravel this 65 million year old extinction mystery it is worth remembering that, if it had not happened, we would not be here to investigate it at all. For it was the demise of the dinosaurs, and the huge gap that their departure left in the ecosystem, that allowed the mammals to evolve rapidly. They soon dominated the land and took to the sea and the air. Eventually, about 4 million years ago, the earliest ancestors of Man appeared.

DINOSAURS

8 The first dinosaur was named over 150 years ago. The subsequent history of dinosaur discovery has featured extra-ordinary people, unexpected finds, and heroic achievements.

ND PEOPLE 8

Above all it is the story of how scientists have struggled to interpret scraps of evidence dug from the ground to understand the most amazing animals ever to live on Earth.

There were no human beings on Earth during the dinosaur era. Despite what you see at the movie theater, the last dinosaur had been dead for at least 65 million years before the first *Homo sapiens* appeared on the scene. Yet in the short century and a half since dinosaurs were first discovered (or perhaps we should say recognized, since people had been discovering their fossilized remains for hundreds of years without knowing what they were), dinosaurs have fascinated scientists and the general public. Why? What is the attraction? Why are you, for example, reading this book? To answer these questions we first need to trace the steps by which dinosaurs came to be recognized, and how each step transformed people's understanding of the prehistoric world.

Dinosaur fossils have been weathering out of the rocks for millions of years. In ancient China they were thought to be the bones of dragons and were prized for their magic and medicinal powers. In fact, the very first description of a dinosaur fossil find comes from a book by the Chinese scholar Chang Qu, writing around AD 300, where he tells of the discovery of dragon bones at Wucheng in what is now Sichuan province. There are also records of American Indians discovering the bones of "giant buffalo" that were thought to give the braves good luck during the hunt. These too were probably dinosaur fossils.

In England there are a number of old books and museum collections that contain pictures, descriptions, and specimens of what we now know to be dinosaur fossils. The most famous is the description, by Robert Plot, of the end of a gigantic thigh bone from Oxfordshire which was first thought to belong to an elephant brought to England by the Romans, and later to be part of a giant human. His picture of the specimen strongly suggests that it was, in fact, from

the meat-eating dinosaur *Megalosaurus*. In 1820 fossil bones found in the Connecticut Valley were described as human remains (they actually belonged to the early dinosaur *Anchisaurus*). Between 1802 and 1860 literally thousands of dinosaur trackway fossils were collected in the same area, first by

A GIANT HUMAN? Described by Robert Plot in 1676 as belonging to a giant human, this is the knee end of a thigh bone of *Megalosaurus*. It was later named, in 1763, by R. Brookes as *Scrotum humanum*, the genitals of a giant man.

Plinny Moody and later by Professor Edward Hitchcock, under the impression they were the prints of giant birds. Indeed, Professor Hitchcock had a whole museum built at Amherst College to house his bird footprint collection and published books describing the prehistoric bird-filled landscape.

With such evidence before them, why did scientists fail to recognize these fossils for what they were? Most people in Europe and America at this time accepted the traditional Christian teaching that the world was made by God in seven days and that all life started in the Garden of Eden. The seventeenth century biblical scholar Archbishop Ussher had added up the ages of all the different prophets and patriarchs mentioned in the Bible, and concluded that the creation event took place in 4004 BC. The idea of extinct species of animals did not fit with these religious convictions. Why would God go to all the trouble of creating creatures and then let them die out?

Hard proof had been coming to light that the Earth's rocks were many

(*Previous spread*) A GIFT DINOSAUR. Andrew Carnegie presenting a plaster cast of *Diplodocus carnegiei* to The Natural History Museum, London, in May 1905.

DRAGON BONES. *Left:* In ancient China dinosaur bones were thought to be the remains of dead dragons and were ground up for medicine and magic potions.

THE FIRST RECORDED FOSSIL FIND. *Right:* Written over 1700 years ago, this account of a dragon bone find is the earliest written description of a dinosaur fossil.

millions of years older than the biblical date suggested and that some of these rocks contained the fossil remains of animals. This was controversial enough on its own, but the idea that prehistoric giant reptiles had inhabited the Earth millions of years before Man was simply unacceptable. The work of the earliest dinosaur scientists thus not only shows brilliant deduction based on minimal fossil evidence, but also their intellectual courage in proposing extraordinary ideas about the Earth's prehistory that radically challenged the accepted thinking of the day.

GIDEON AND MARY MANTELL

The first person to recognize that huge reptiles had existed in the remote past was Gideon Mantell. Living in the town of Lewes, England, Mantell was a doctor with many patients in the surrounding countryside. He was also an enthusiastic amateur paleontologist and often used his trips from one patient to another to scan the fossil rich Sussex countryside for specimens. The story is that, one day in the spring of 1822, Dr Mantell visited a patient with his wife Mary Ann. While he was in the house she strolled up and down the road, which was being repaired by workmen. A pile of stone from one of the local quarries had been dumped at the roadside and among the broken pieces she noticed something shining. She picked up the pieces of rock and saw that they contained some unusual fossil teeth. Mary Ann Mantell's decision to hold on to the specimens and show them to her husband was one of the most significant events in the whole history of dinosaur study.

Gideon Mantell instantly recognized that these were most remarkable fossils. He could tell that the teeth were from a plant-eater because they were blunt and had been worn down on one side by constant chewing. They must also have come from a very large animal indeed and looked, he thought, very like the incisor of an elephant or rhinoceros. With the help of the men who had delivered the stone, he tracked the source of the fossils to a quarry in the Tilgate Forest. Here the mystery of the teeth deepened, because the age of the rocks in the quarry, about 130 million years, showed that the teeth came from the Mesozoic Era — the age of reptiles when no large mammals (and certainly no elephants or rhinoceros) lived on Earth. Was it possible that these teeth belonged to a giant prehistoric reptile, hundreds of times bigger than any other so far discovered? We can imagine Mantell wrestling with this extraordinary idea, alone in his study in Lewes.

Mantell was convinced that his find was important, but how could he find out more? He sent the teeth and some fossil foot bones found in the same quarry to two of the most famous scientists of the day, Baron Georges Cuvier in Paris and Dr William Buckland, the Professor of Geology at Oxford University. Their response was hardly encouraging. Cuvier wrote back to say that the teeth came from a rhinoceros and the foot bones from a hippopotamus. Buckland thought the teeth were from a large fish or much more recent mammal whose remains had been accidentally washed into the old rock of the quarry. Buckland even went so far as to warn Mantell, in a friendly way, not to publish a description of the bones.

Despite this reaction Mantell persisted. He began searching through collections of ancient and modern skeletons for anything that looked like the teeth and might give him an idea about the animal they belonged to. At the Hunterian Museum of the Royal College of Surgeons in London he was directed toward the vital clue, the skeleton of a modern iguana from South America, by a visiting anatomist, Samuel Stutchbury. There, in its much smaller jaw, were virtual mirror images of the fossil teeth he had discovered. The same broad diamond shape, the same ridged edges. His prehistoric teeth were indeed from a reptile, some form of giant lizard, possibly like a huge iguana. In 1825, three years after his wife's first discovery, Mantell published a description of the find and the name of the animal, *Iguanodon* ("iguana tooth").

Mantell had to wait another nine years before making any significant progress on *Iguanodon*. In 1834 a large number of *Iguanodon* bones were discovered embedded in a slab of rock in a Maidstone, England, quarry. The quarry owner demanded the high price of £25

GIDEON MANTELL. The first person to recognize the existence of extinct giant reptiles. These *Iguanodon* teeth puzzled Mantell for three years until he saw the jaw of a modern iguana lizard and made the connection between its teeth and those of the plant-eating *Iguanodon*.

for the specimen and eventually some of Mantell's friends clubbed together to buy it for him. Now at last he could get a real picture of the size and shape of the animal he had named. His early sketches, based on the Maidstone discovery, show a crouching, lizardlike creature with a spike on its nose — hardly an accurate representation of *Iguanodon* as we know it today, but a huge leap in understanding at the time. The town of Maidstone in Kent, England, bears *Iguanodon* on its coat of arms as a tribute to the importance of this discovery.

BUCKLAND AND OWEN

In the study of dinosaurs (or any other organism) it is the date of publication of a specimen's description and name that counts as the moment of its official recognition. According to this rule, the first person to describe and name a dinosaur (even though he did not use the word) was not Mantell but Dr William Buckland, who published a description of the jaw of an animal that he called *Megalosaurus* in 1824, the year before Mantell's piece about *Iguanodon* appeared in print.

William Buckland was an eccentric clergyman (he later became Dean of Westminster Abbey) and geologist who had jackals in his living room and a bear in the hallway of his house. The bear also used to ride behind him on his horse and make frequent raids on the candy counter of the local village post office. He was brilliant as well as eccentric and a well-known popular writer on scientific subjects ranging from the geological structure of the Alps to Ice Age mammals. His work on *Megalosaurus* was based on the study of

THE "MANTELL-PIECE." *Above:* "Now for three months hard work at night with my chisel," wrote the excited Gideon Mantell when this slab containing *Iguanodon* bones was delivered to his house in 1834 (spare a thought for his wife and children)!

Left: His early pen and ink sketch shows how lizardlike he thought *Iguanodon* to be. It was based on the only skeleton fragments then known and consequently was very inaccurate. For example, the thumb spike was mistaken for a nose horn and the ilium is drawn at the wrong angle.

UNDER JAW AND TEETH OF MEGALOSAURUS.

DEAN WILLIAM BUCKLAND. The first person to describe and name a dinosaur, *Megalosaurus*, which was based on remains including a lower jaw. A brilliant and eccentric man, he became Dean of Westminster Abbey and had his umbrella engraved with the words "Stolen from Dean Buckland."

the fossil jaw and bones that had been housed in the Oxford Museum since at least 1818. His published description of them is full and accurate, leading Baron Cuvier to estimate that *Megalosaurus* might have been up to 40 feet long, although he thought the remains belonged to a voracious marine reptile.

In the years following the publications of Mantell and Buckland, other giant reptile remains from the Mesozoic Era gradually came to light in England and Europe, and by 1840 nine such reptiles had been named. At this point the figure of Richard Owen enters the story. He was one of the foremost Victorian

scientists and a world expert in the field of animal anatomy. He was a member of numerous committees and scientific organizations, a close friend of Queen Victoria (who presented him with a house in Richmond Park, London) and the first Superintendent of The Natural History Museum in London. One of his many appointments involved the dissection of animals that had died at London Zoo, so he had good first-hand experience of unusual species and how their bodies were constructed.

Owen made an extensive study of all the giant reptile fossils available and came to the conclusion that they were not

related to any modern reptiles. If they were not ancient versions of crocodiles or lizards, what were they? He reached the conclusion that three of them, *Megalosaurus*, *Iguanodon*, and *Hylaeosaurus*, were prehistoric reptiles of enormous size belonging to a previously unrecognized group of animals he called Dinosauria from the Greek *deinos*, meaning "terrible" and *sauros*, meaning "lizard." Owen first announced this name at the British Association for the Advancement of Science annual meeting in Plymouth, England, in 1841. It was a truly remarkable piece of deduction on Owen's part. Today, a scientist considering announcing a new animal group would expect to study hundreds of specimens in microscopic detail to check and recheck the facts. Owen had the fragmentary remains of three quite different animals. He did not even really know what those animals looked like, as we can tell by looking at the famous life-sized restorations he supervised in 1854. These models, which can still be seen at Crystal Palace Park in London, show heavy, four-legged creatures with the build and stance of an elephant or rhinoceros. As we now know, these were very inaccurate, yet Owen managed to correctly identify dinosaurs as a single group and define several of the characteristics by which they are recognized to this day.

Over the last 150 years many brilliant people have found and named many dinosaurs. But only Gideon Mantell, William Buckland, and Richard Owen can be said to have "discovered" them. Owen's contribution was an intellectual one (he certainly never went digging for bones), building the idea of a new group of giant prehistoric reptiles from

DINNER IN THE IGUANODON MODEL, AT THE CRYSTAL PALACE, SYDENHAM.

RICHARD OWEN. *Below:* Inventor of the word "dinosaur" and the first person to recognize them as a distinct group. His designs for life-sized models, constructed by the sculptor Benjamin Waterhouse Hawkins, caused a public sensation when they were exhibited at Crystal Palace, London, in 1854. *Above:* This contemporary *Illustrated London News* picture shows a dinner in Owen's honor being given inside the half-completed *Iguanodon*.

fragments of fossil bone. His brilliant thinking, Buckland's skilled observation, and Mantell's courage to press ahead despite discouragement, make these men unique in the history of dinosaur study.

FIRST FINDS IN THE USA

Soon after the elephantine dinosaur models were displayed at Crystal Palace, a spectacular dinosaur find in New Jersey, cast doubt on the whole basis of Richard Owen's view of how dinosaurs looked. In 1858, William Parker Foulke was staying in the town of Haddonfield when he fell into conversation with a local farmer. The farmer told how, twenty years earlier, he had dug up some huge fossil bones from a marl pit on his land and given them away to friends as souvenirs. Excited by the prospect of

finding something unusual, Foulke gained the farmer's permission to excavate the marl pit and hired a team of local diggers. They soon unearthed a large number of fossil bones and Foulke sent at once for the famous scientist Dr Joseph Leidy who was a Professor at the University of Philadelphia. Leidy studied the bones over the next few months and then published a description of them, naming the dinosaur *Hadrosaurus foulkii* (Foulke's heavy lizard). From the well-preserved leg bones Leidy was able to deduce that this dinosaur, which was in many ways similar to *Iguanodon*, stood upright in a birdlike posture, and was not a four-legged plodder as Richard Owen had suggested. Once again, and not for the last time, the accepted view of dinosaurs was being challenged by the evidence of a new find. For the next

twenty years this debate continued with each side finding and describing dinosaurs that seemed to prove their point. The fossil skeletons of the agile meat-eaters *Dryptosaurus* (formerly *Laelaps*) and *Compsognathus* were cited by one group as clear evidence of two-legged stance, while Owen's descriptions of the stegosaur *Omosaurus* (now called *Dacentrurus*) and the heavily armored ankylosaur *Scelidosaurus* pointed in the other direction. Both groups were right, of course, as we now know from many finds of two- and four-legged dinosaurs.

THE BERNISSART FIND

The next major world dinosaur find was to resolve this and many other questions. In April 1878 some coal miners in Bernissart, Belgium, found themselves hacking through a giant fossil skeleton some 1050 feet below ground level. They informed the mine managers who quickly handed over the supervision of the excavation of the bones to scientists from the Royal Museum of Natural History in Brussels.

What the miners had discovered was no less than a "mass grave" of *Iguanodon* with nearly thirty complete skeletons, many of them preserved intact in the positions in which they died. More remarkable still, the fossils were not preserved in horizontal strata through the rock but in a vertical column of clay over 100 feet high that cut through the layers of shale and coal. How had this come about? Careful work over the next three years led scientists to believe that this had been a deep, narrow ravine in the prehistoric landscape. It was initially suggested that a herd of *Iguanodon* had fallen into it and been covered by layers of mud swept down by heavy rains.

However, since the skeletons were found at different levels in the pit, it is now believed that the accumulation took place over a period of many years.

Piece by piece, block by numbered block, hundreds of bones were dug out of the mine and transported back to Brussels for study and assembly by the newly appointed "assistant naturalist" Louis Dollo. This was an opportunity for the kind of dinosaur study that had never been possible before and very seldom since. Instead of a single animal Dollo had dozens of complete specimens to compare. He was able to prove conclusively that *Iguanodon* was two-legged, that the spike which Mantell and Owen had put on its nose was actually a thumb, and that the latticelike ossified tendons along the spine were designed to give strength to the back and tail. He used the mass of fossil evidence to work out the position and size of muscles and the way that *Iguanodon* moved. At the same time he was busy reconstructing and mounting the Bernissart skeletons for display in the Brussels museum. About thirty of them can be seen there today, held in vast glass enclosures.

Louis Dollo's work on the Bernissart *Iguanodon* in many ways laid the foundation for the modern study of dinosaurs as living animals in a real environment. In addition to his study of the bones themselves he looked at the fossil remains of other animals buried with the *Iguanodon* skeletons, including several different species of crocodiles and turtles. He also studied the plant fossils and the way the sediments had been turned into rock, to try and construct as accurate a picture as possible of the dinosaurs and how they lived.

Louis Dollo. *Top:* Dollo spent most of his working life studying the *Iguanodon* skeletons found at Bernissart, Belgium. His work took dinosaur study to a new level of detail and accuracy. *Opposite:* The Bernissart skeletons were reconstructed in a church, the only large enough space, and were then transferred to the Brussels museum (*above*).

COPE AND MARSH

At the time of the Bernissart discoveries, dinosaur study in the USA was dominated by the personalities of two men — Edward Drinker Cope and Othniel Charles Marsh. Both were distinguished American academics, both brilliant, both hugely energetic in seeking and describing dinosaurs, and both hated each other. Their rivalry is one of the great legends of dinosaur science and was largely responsible for what has come to be called the "American Dinosaur Rush."

Why did Cope and Marsh detest each other? As late as 1868 there are records of them spending a friendly week together exploring the Haddonfield area (where *Hadrosaurus foulkii* had been found), yet two years later they were bitter enemies. One story is that Cope had described a new prehistoric sea

EDWARD DRINKER COPE

OTHNIEL CHARLES MARSH

COPE AND MARSH. Bitter rivals during their lifetimes, the names of these two great American paleontologists will remain forever linked. Their rivalry certainly drove each of them to make extraordinary attempts to locate new dinosaur remains. Between them they named nearly 130 new dinosaurs, scouring North America for new species to put them ahead in the "Dinosaur Rush."

"DIPLODOCUS CARNEGII": DR. W. J. HOLLAND SETTING UP THE DINOSAURIAN REPTILE AT THE NATURAL HISTORY MUSEUM

THE MILLIONAIRE'S DINOSAUR. Millionaire industrialist Andrew Carnegie financed an expedition to excavate spectacular dinosaur fossils in Wyoming. One of them was named in his honor, *Diplodocus carnegiei*, and he then paid for plaster casts to be made and sent to museums around the world. In London there was great public interest in the dinosaur when it was presented to the Trustees of The Natural History Museum (previously The British Museum (Natural History)) in May 1905.

reptile called *Elasmosaurus*, drawing particular attention to its strange backbone. Marsh came to see the fossil and pointed out that Cope had actually reconstructed it back to front with the skull at the end of its tail. Cope never forgave him for this humiliation. Whatever the reason, the rivalry between them was well established by 1877 when two schoolmasters, independently exploring the Colorado area, found large and exciting new dinosaur fossils. One sent his finds to Cope, the other to Marsh.

The result was an explosion of dinosaur exploration as Cope and Marsh hired teams of diggers to excavate the areas where the fossils had been found. Cope's patch seemed to have bigger and better bones, but later in 1877 Marsh had a stroke of luck that put him firmly ahead in the dinosaur race. In a mysterious letter, two men calling themselves "Harlow and Edwards" told him that they had discovered giant bones at a secret location in Wyoming. "Harlow and Edwards" turned out to be two railroad workers. What they had actually discovered was a 7 mile stretch of Jurassic fossil-bearing rock at Como Bluff alongside the Union Pacific Railroad. Marsh signed an agreement with them and they began shipping bones back to him by the ton. Naturally, the Como Bluff area attracted Cope's attention as soon as he came to know what was going on there, and there are stories of clashes between the two rival teams as they searched for the best dinosaur remains.

By the end of the 1880s both Marsh and Cope had shifted their attentions to the Cretaceous fossil beds of western North America. Both of them had, in fact,

made explorations here earlier in their careers. Marsh had named two dinosaurs from these rocks and Cope had undertaken an amazing expedition to Montana in 1876, the year when Chief Sitting Bull wiped out General Custer's forces at the battle of Little Big Horn. The Judith River fossil beds were in the heart of Sioux territory, and the local people warned Cope against venturing out. He insisted it was safe, however, and in the end his only encounters with the Indians were friendly. One of his party describes how Cope used to entertain them by taking out his false teeth and showing them around. By 1892 both Cope and Marsh were back in the area again searching for specimens from the very last years of the dinosaur era.

Read any book on dinosaurs and the names of Cope and Marsh come up again and again. Their rivalry certainly spurred each of them into huge efforts to find new dinosaurs. Between them they named almost 130 new species, many from virtually complete fossil skeletons, transforming the understanding of dinosaur life. Louis Dollo had shown how dinosaurs could be studied as living animals based on the detailed study of one species. Cope and Marsh revealed the dinosaur world as a varied community of extraordinary reptiles. The contribution of these three men to dinosaur science has never been equaled.

DISCOVERIES ON EVERY CONTINENT

The first important dinosaur find in Canada was made in 1884 when the skull of the large meat-eater *Albertosaurus* was unearthed in the Red Deer River Valley in Alberta. Various

attempts were made to explore this rugged terrain, but it was the American Barnum Brown who mounted the first full-scale expedition in 1910, using a huge, flat-bottomed barge. This acted as a base camp as he floated down the river, stopping at likely points to search and excavate. The barge was also an ideal means of transporting the fossils themselves, which would certainly have been damaged by a long, bumpy horse and cart ride to the railroad. Brown worked for several summers along the valley finding superbly preserved skeletons of dinosaurs such as *Corythosaurus*, *Styracosaurus*, and *Centrosaurus*. Over many years the Red Deer River had worn a valley through the fossil-bearing rock, exposing dinosaur bones at many levels along its steep banks. The valley rocks span millions of years of prehistory, allowing Brown to collect specimens that showed how dinosaur life in the area had evolved over time.

In 1907 a German engineer, working in what is now Tanzania, came across the fossil bones of a giant dinosaur just outside the village of Tendaguru. Word of the find soon reached the director of the Berlin museum who set about raising the money for a full-scale excavation. Money was certainly needed, for this was to be a dinosaur excavation of a scale and type never before attempted. Tendaguru was 40 miles from the coast — four days' march through jungle. There were no roads, no machines, and no transport. At the height of the excavation over 500 local workers with their families were living on the site. It was a complete town that had to be provided with food, water, sanitation, building materials, and medicines. The

DINOSAURS GIANTS. No excavations on the scale of Tendaguru, Tanzania, had been undertaken before. Among the giant dinosaurs found there between 1909 and 1911 was this *Brachiosaurus*. Displayed at the Humboldt Museum in Berlin *(left)*, it remains the world's largest mounted skeleton. *Above:* This enormous shoulder blade was excavated by an expedition from London's Natural History Museum in the late 1920s.

statistics compiled by the expedition organizers tell their own story about the effort involved. In the first three years (1909–1911) 4300 loads of fossil bones were sent from the excavation to the port of Lindi. Every load was carried by a team of porters who made a total of 5400 round trips. In the end over 250 tons of fossil and rock were carried away from Tendaguru. The finds were certainly extensive and spectacular. They included the massive sauropod *Brachiosaurus*, the largest complete skeleton ever found, the plated stegosaur *Kentrosaurus*, and the fast running two-legged plant-eater *Dryosaurus*.

The discovery of dinosaurs in Mongolia was almost an accident. In 1922, the American Museum of Natural History decided to mount an expedition to the Gobi Desert to search for early mammal fossils and the origins of prehistoric Man. Roy Chapman Andrews was in charge of the practical arrangements and devised a plan whereby camel caravans plodded slowly through the desert carrying tons of gasoline, oil, food, and supplies. Meanwhile the fossil searchers covered hundreds of miles each day, zigzagging across the open terrain in cars and tracking their way back to prearranged meeting points using a nautical sextant and compass. The system worked beautifully but the scientists found very few human or mammal remains. Instead, in a series of expeditions between 1922 and 1925, they came across the skeletons of new and spectacular dinosaurs, including *Oviraptor* and *Saurornithoides*, and the first dinosaur nests and eggs, belonging to *Protoceratops*.

The US expeditions did a small amount of dinosaur exploration in China on their way to and from the Gobi Desert, and a Russian group excavated the Chinese hadrosaurid *Mandschurosaurus* (now called *Gilmoreosaurus*) in 1917. But in 1933 Professor Yang Zhong-jian was put in charge of Chinese dinosaur

YANG ZHONG-JIAN. *Above:* CC Young (as he is better known in the West) was responsible for Chinese dinosaur exploration for forty years. *Below:* Finds of giant sauropods like *Mamenchisaurus* proved that related dinosaur species existed at the same time in quite different parts of the world.

ROY CHAPMAN ANDREWS. Seen here in the Gobi Desert with a nest of dinosaur eggs, Chapman Andrews was not himself a paleontologist. His genius lay in organizing dinosaur hunting expeditions to some of the remotest parts of the world using cars, camels, and porters.

CHANGING VIEWS. This sequence of *Iguanodon* models shows clearly how scientific thinking about dinosaurs has developed over the years.

Waterhouse Hawkins, 1853, showed *Iguanodon* as a heavily built quadruped with its thumb spike mistaken for a nose horn.

Vernon Edwards, 1940s, basing his model on the Bernissart skeletons depicted *Iguanodon* in a strictly bipedal kangaroolike posture.

Recent studies show that the weight of *Iguanodon*'s body was counterbalanced by the heavy tail and that it was able to move on two or four legs.

exploration and, over the next forty years, was responsible for some of the most remarkable discoveries of this century. Dinosaurs from virtually every group have been found, including the amazingly long-necked *Mamenchisaurus*, the plated stegosaur *Tuojiangosaurus*, and several hadrosaurs.

Today, work on dinosaurs goes on around the world with discoveries on every continent. Each new find expands what we know about the prehistoric world, sometimes confirming and sometimes overturning the accepted thinking about a particular species or aspect of dinosaur life. Finds are made in the most far-flung locations, such as the *Iguanodon* footprints discovered on the Arctic island of West Spitzbergen. At the other end of the world in Antarctica, an ankylosaur and a small plant-eater similar to *Hypsilophodon* have been discovered in the last few years.

Some finds occur just a few hundred yards from roads and houses, as with the remarkable story of *Baryonyx* (see Chapter 9). At the same time, existing fossil-rich sites are being further studied and excavated and new techniques of laboratory study are yielding more information from fossils that have sat in museum storerooms for decades. New ideas are being published continually, new research undertaken, and new theories discussed. Dinosaur exploration takes many forms — in the field, under the microscope, in the laboratory, and the museum display gallery. But above all the search goes on in the minds of dinosaur scientists, amateur and professional, whose work takes them step by step nearer to an understanding of the dinosaurs and their world.

AN ENDLESS ATTRACTION

Dinosaurs have always fascinated the general public. Only fourteen years after Richard Owen first invented the word his life-sized restorations were attracting huge crowds into Crystal Palace. Today, a new dinosaur exhibition will guarantee queues around the block for any museum in the world. More than anything else people want to see what dinosaurs looked like, and the work of skilled dinosaur illustrators has always been in high demand. Some details about how illustrators work are given in Chapter 9, but it is very important to remember that each picture is only as accurate as the scientific information that the artist is given.

Alongside the popular interest in dinosaur science has come the extensive use of dinosaurs in fiction and adventure stories. Dinosaurs are a gift to authors and comic strip artists because they create an instant adventure, being big, dangerous, and liable to fight anything that moves. They can also be portrayed as slow and stupid, allowing the human heroes to outwit them and triumph in the end. Scientific accuracy plays little part in these stories. Once the humans and dinosaurs have somehow been brought together, then dinosaurs from any and every era are likely to appear alongside each other displaying the kinds of behavior that can make even the most broad-minded paleontologist howl with anguish.

The appearance of dinosaurs in feature films and cartoons, often portraying them as comic and endearing, has added a whole new dimension to the task of illustration. The very first use of dinosaurs in moving cartoon form,

THE FLINTSTONES. Contrary to this popular image, dinosaurs and early Man were separated by 61 million years.

"Gertie the dinosaur" by Winsor McCay in 1914, used just this sort of technique to appeal to movie audiences. A number of techniques to show dinosaurs moving were tried in the early days, many of them pioneered by the American special effects experts Willis O'Brian and later Ray Harryhausen. From moving models to trick optics and remote controlled robots, the quest for realistic screen dinosaurs gets ever more complex (and expensive).

While dinosaurs are an accepted fact of prehistoric life for most people, there are those who find it hard to accept the scientific facts about their existence. Such people usually also reject the whole concept of evolution, insisting instead on religious beliefs about the creation of the whole world as a single, divinely organized event. This has led to some interesting interpretations of dinosaur fossil evidence. In one location in Texas, a set of sauropod trackways is said by many "creationists" to show the footprints of human beings walking beside the dinosaur. This is clear evidence, they claim, that dinosaurs and people did indeed live at the same time. Even today dinosaurs can be an issue of intense controversy and passionately held beliefs.

Which brings us back to the question that started this chapter. Why are people so interested in dinosaurs? Firstly, because dinosaurs were such extraordinary animals. They have something of the fairytale dragon or monster about them that is exciting, frightening, and fascinating all at the same time. Secondly, they are all dead, so we do not have to worry about what they might do to us or what we are doing to them — a depressing anxiety with the more extraordinary animals in today's world. Most importantly, dinosaurs are so popular because there is so much still to find out about them. Every new fossil find has the potential to challenge the accepted wisdom about a dinosaur species or even about dinosaurs in general. What if fossilized skin were found with the color somehow preserved? What if an even bigger meat-eater than *Tyrannosaurus* were discovered? Or a family of *Tyrannosaurus* hatchlings? Or evidence of feathers on a *Deinonychus*? Anyone could make such a find. Amateur fossil collectors are the eyes and hands of dinosaur scientists around the world. No other branch of science offers such a potential opportunity for non-experts to participate or such exciting rewards for doing so.

What type of work do paleontologists do? The journey from first finding a new dinosaur fossil to putting its skeleton on display can take many years. In between lie painstaking hours of preparation, restoration, academic study and writing. The skills of many people are employed to create as detailed a picture as possible of the living animal.

S tudying dinosaurs requires an extraordinary range of skills. A good paleontologist must combine the qualities of an explorer, an archaeologist, a detective, and an artist, as well as having a detailed knowledge of animal structure and function. So what do these dinosaur scientists do? How do you study a dinosaur?

First you have to find one, or rather find its fossilized remains. Fossils are only formed in certain kinds of sedimentary rock (see Chapter 1), and there are only a few places in the world, some very remote, where that rock is exposed at the surface. The good news is that new dinosaur fossils are being exposed all the time as wind and water wear away the covering rock. Some dinosaur discoveries are made quite by chance when amateur collectors explore old and new fossil beds. Others are planned, usually when a museum or university mounts a full-scale expedition to a carefully chosen site, complete with trucks, generators, and tons of digging, surveying, and packing materials.

THE PALEONTOLOGIST AT WORK

The purpose of every expedition is to excavate new dinosaur skeletons and bring them back to the laboratory for study. Half a hillside of rock may have to be removed, yet the fossil bones themselves must be treated with the utmost care. The paleontologist may use a pneumatic drill one day and a putty knife and soft paintbrush the next. In the final stages it is quite common to cut out the fossil, still embedded in rock, and pack it up in plaster of Paris bandages or polyurethane foam for transportation. It is vital, however, that a detailed survey is made before anything is removed from the site. The survey notes the exact position of all the bones when found, and can prove invaluable in later study of the dinosaur skeleton. The lumps of fossil rock are then taken away, usually in trucks, although camels, mules, and elephants have also been used!

Back in the laboratory the paleontologist–explorer turns into a paleontologist–preparator, whose task is to remove the rest of the surrounding rock, called the matrix, from the fossil bones. These may have been broken or crushed during fossilization, so the matrix must be taken away very gently to avoid losing any fragments. The one thing in the paleontologist's favor is that the matrix is often (but not always!) a softer rock than the fossil inside.

A typical lump of rock, fresh in from the excavation, will undergo a strict preparation process. Large pieces of the matrix are first removed with hammer and chisel, a diamond-bladed pneumatic saw, or even a shot-blaster, leaving a thin coating of rock round the fossil. There is now a choice. If the matrix is made of limestone it can be dissolved away with a solution of acetic or formic acid, allowing the acid-resistant fossil bone to

FOSSIL FINDS. *Below:* Dinosaur discoveries have been made on every continent. Some of the fossil sites are very remote indeed, such as northern Alaska and Antarctica.

(*Previous spread*) DEATH POSE. A scale model of the British dinosaur *Baryonyx* based on years of work by scientists at The Natural History Museum, London.

THE *BARYONYX* STORY: DISCOVERY. In January 1983 Mr William Walker, an amateur collector, found this huge fossil claw bone in a Surrey, England, clay pit (shown here actual size). Paleontologists at The Natural History Museum in London identified it as belonging to a large and unusual meat-eating dinosaur. No one yet suspected that Mr Walker had made the most important European dinosaur discovery this century.

emerge gradually. This technique is particularly good for small, delicate fossils but it is very slow.

If the matrix is very thick or insoluble in acid, the shot blaster may well be used. This is housed in a huge steel and reinforced glass cabinet in which cast iron shot or plastic pellets about the size of sugar grains are fired at the fossil rock, with a noise like a violent hailstorm. Great skill is needed to manipulate the rock during blasting so that the fossil bones are exposed without damage. As each part of the fossil appears it is painted with a coat of latex rubber to prevent it being eaten away by the pellets. It is rarely possible to deal with the whole matrix by blasting, but it can rapidly remove most of the rock "coat" and reduce the rest to a few millimeters thickness. Sometimes thick rock is removed by cutting grooves in it with an air-powered saw and then chipping away the ridges in between. This process can be repeated several times. In this way the rock is removed in controlled layers.

It is now that the really painstaking work begins. With a fine air-powered engraver, dentist's drill, scalpel, and needle, the paleontologist removes the last of the matrix (sometimes as little as one grain of rock at a time), strengthening the fossil with fast-drying resin as the bone is uncovered. Remember, dinosaur bones are not conveniently smooth and straight. They have hollows, holes, curves, cracks, and little sticking out bits that can drive you mad. A week's intensive work under the stereo microscope may do no more than expose the details of one vertebra (*Diplodocus* had over ninety), and it can take years of labor to prepare a whole skeleton. Every dinosaur museum in the world has dozens of mysterious plaster of Paris packages on its store shelves — untouched fossils just waiting for preparation, "when there's time to get round to it."

SCIENTIFIC STUDY

By now the paleontologist has changed roles again and is beginning the academic study of the fossil specimens. The first stage is to identify just what all the pieces are. It is very rare that a dinosaur skeleton is found complete with all the bones helpfully in the right place. Pieces of the dead animal may have been carried off by scavengers, washed away by a river, re-arranged, or destroyed as the surrounding rock shifted over millions of years. The result is a three-dimensional jigsaw puzzle which may have any number of pieces missing or broken, and from which a reconstruction is attempted without a guiding picture.

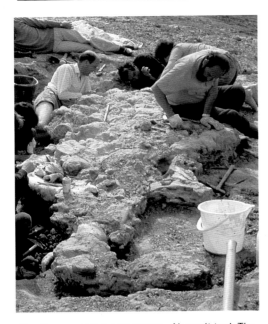

THE *BARYONYX* STORY: EXCAVATION. *Above:* It took The Natural History Museum team three weeks to excavate the skeleton. Some fossil bones were loose in the clay, but most were encased in hard blocks of iron-impregnated siltstone. Each was separated from its neighbor and packed in a protective jacket for transportation. *Right:* Before leaving the site the exact position of every block and bone was meticulously noted by the paleontologists on this survey map.

METRES

■ skull
□ lower jaw
☆ loose teeth
▲ cervical vertebrae
△ dorsal vertebrae
▼ caudal vertebrae
▽ ribs
▶ abdominal ribs
◆ pectoral girdle
● forelimb
◇ pelvic girdle
○ hind limb

bone might read like this:

". . . the long strongly opisthocoelous cervical vertebrae with short neural spines, with well-developed epipophyses, and with ends of the centra not 'offset' so that when they are correctly apposed . . ."

This is pretty heavy going, particularly when you consider that a large skeleton may have more than 300 individual bones to describe.

The technique for illustrating bones has not changed much since Victorian times, with pen and ink being most often used. Some paleontologists are superb scientific artists as well and do all their own drawing. Others work with skilled illustrators to give a view of all the bones from several angles. A detailed photographic record, sometimes stereoscopic, is made at the same time.

The process of identifying and describing the fossil bones often throws up as many questions as answers for the paleontologist. It is now time to tackle these questions using a mixture of scientific principles, deduction, comparison with other fossils and with modern animals, and sometimes, inspired guesswork. For example, how do all the pieces of the bone jigsaw actually fit together? If the paleontologist is lucky there may be up to half the complete

Just like doing a jigsaw puzzle, the paleontologist starts with the important pieces — the ones that will give most information straight away. Skulls and teeth rank first among these so called "diagnostic" bones. Each main group of dinosaurs had a very different skull structure, and it is often possible to find out a great deal about your new discovery from quite small pieces of skull. Teeth give you information about the dinosaur's diet, and vertebrae are also useful, again because each dinosaur group had its own particular kind.

The paleontologist's work at this stage is very slow and careful. Each piece of bone must be described and illustrated in detail. Part of the description of a single

THE *BARYONYX* STORY: PREPARATION. A shot-blaster eats away at a block of rock. Most of the siltstone matrix surrounding the fossil bones was removed in this way, with power chisels and diamond-bladed saws as backup. Some blocks contained several bones or parts of bones. The exposed fossil bone was coated with latex rubber to prevent damage during shot-blasting.

skeleton to work with. Quite a few gaps can be filled by modeling from the bones that are present. A right rib, for example, can be carefully modeled as a "mirror image" of the corresponding left rib. If you have three toes from one foot and one from the other you can use them as the basis for making up a complete set for both. But if a great number of bones are lacking, you have to fill them in by scientific comparison with the most similar dinosaurs and by using the site survey map to see how the skeleton lay when it was found.

You can see now how important the site survey is. Careless collecting and surveying can lead to some amazing mistakes at the reconstruction stage. Bones from two different dinosaurs found in the same place can be assembled as one, or pieces fitted into the wrong place entirely. Indeed, until very recently the original skeleton of *Apatosaurus* (discovered by Othniel Marsh in 1877) was restored with a *Camarasaurus* skull. This was because an isolated skull and headless skeleton had been found quite close together and it was assumed, following Marsh's notes,

THE *BARYONYX* STORY: MORE PREPARATION. Working under a stereo microscope, a scientist scrapes away the last traces of matrix with an air-powered engraver. Quick drying resins were used to strengthen the fragile bone as it appeared. Every detail of the new fossil was precious because of the information it could give about the dinosaur. The fully prepared pieces were placed in air-conditioned storage to await detailed study.

THE *BARYONYX* STORY: RECONSTRUCTION. It is often necessary to model pieces of missing skeleton or make casts of the fossil bones for detailed study. Modeling is done with softened wax or modeling clay, gradually adding the missing pieces to the original. Molds are made from silicone rubber and may consist of several interlocked pieces. Bone-colored resin and glass fiber are used for the casts, which are exact replicas of the originals.

THE *BARYONYX* STORY: DESCRIPTION AND ASSEMBLY. The white areas are the parts of the dinosaur found during the excavation, about 60 percent of the whole skeleton. By carefully examining and describing each fossil bone, paleontologists were able to fill in the missing parts and assemble a picture of the complete animal. The dinosaur weighed about 2 tons, was over 30 feet long, 10–13 feet tall, and walked on two legs.

John Holmes-92

that they belonged to each other. It was not until 1975 that this mistake was finally corrected and *Apatosaurus* acquired its proper skull.

If the dinosaur you have discovered is one of an already known species you have the work of other scientists to guide you. This can be no more than a guide, however, since your example may have new pieces or even shed new light about the whole way the animal stood or walked. You need only look at the way our view of *Iguanodon* has changed over the years to see that there is always room for new thinking, even with the best-known dinosaurs. If your discovery is a new species, reconstruction is more challenging still and you must use what you know of other similar dinosaurs as a basis.

With the skeleton assembled as a working drawing, the paleontologist now tries to put the muscle structure in place. There are no such things as fossilized muscles, of course, and even a simple action, like chewing, involves a large number of muscles working together. Comparison with living animals is the only real way to understand this complex aspect of the dinosaur, and a detailed knowledge of modern animal anatomy is essential for every paleontologist.

Finally, the three-dimensional jigsaw puzzle is completed. Each piece of fossil bone is identified and missing pieces filled in where possible. The basic size, shape, and stance of the dinosaur are clear. It may have taken the paleontologist years to get this far, but it is now possible to attempt some further detective work, drawing on all the

THE *BARYONYX* STORY: INTERPRETATION. *Top:* The s-shaped curve of the new dinosaur's jaw was strikingly similar to that of modern fish-eating crocodiles. It also had sixty-four teeth in its lower jaw, twice the number found in other meat-eating dinosaurs. Paleontologists deduced from these features that it must have been a fish-eater. *Bottom:* This idea was later confirmed when fossil scales and teeth of the fish *Lepidotes,* like the one shown here, were found in the area where the stomach would have been.

available evidence to deduce more about how the dinosaur looked and the way it might have lived.

BUILDING UP THE PICTURE
As with any detective, the best place to search for clues is where the body was found. Skilled interpretation of the surrounding rocks can sometimes show the position of cliffs, valleys, and waterways, and whether the dead dinosaur was buried in sand, mud, or river silt. This gives an indication of what the prehistoric location might have looked like, and even what the dinosaur

was doing there. Sometimes the evidence from the rocks is very dramatic. At one site in Utah, a large number of different-sized *Allosaurus* skeletons have been found together (the only mass discovery of large meat-eaters) as well as the remains of different plant-eaters including *Stegosaurus* and *Camarasaurus.* The surrounding rocks show that the area may well have been a natural bog, so presumably one *Allosaurus* was attracted by a stranded plant-eater and became trapped in the sticky ground. Perhaps one by one the other hunters waded in to get a bite of the plant-eater

A FISHING DINOSAUR. *Baryonyx* may have used its large claws to catch large fish such as *Lepidotes* in the rivers and swamps that covered southern England about 120 million years ago.

plant-eaters in the late Cretaceous. Perhaps the comparison of skulls and teeth actually tells this much wider story of dinosaur evolution.

The other key task that the paleontologist must undertake is to work out where an individual species should be placed on the dinosaur "family tree." Many learned and weighty volumes have been written on this subject, but there are basic principles to help sort out the main relationships.

What we need to look for are characteristics that made one kind of dinosaur different from all the others, and characteristics that several species had in common. These characteristics must ideally be really major ones, fundamental to the way the dinosaur is constructed, and not just incidental features. And they must be to do with bones and teeth, since that is all we have left of most dinosaurs. Dinosaur sorting or classifying, therefore, involves looking at each dinosaur and asking a series of "Does it have?" questions about its fossilized skeleton. The more questions you can answer, the better you can narrow down its position on the family tree.

The first question is, "Does it have hips like a bird or like a lizard?" Bird-hipped dinosaurs (which are not related to birds despite the name) belong to the group called Ornithischia and are all plant-eaters. Lizard-hipped dinosaurs belong to Saurischia, a group that contains both plant- and meat-eaters. The diagram shows the kind of further questions that must be asked about the dinosaur, all of them related to teeth, skulls, vertebrae, claws, and so on. Some of them may be

and each other and became stuck themselves, finally suffocating or starving to death. It is possible that this place was a natural hazard for many years, accumulating its remarkable skeleton collection over time.

Detailed study of individual skeletons can lead to other questions about the history of all dinosaurs. An example of this is the skulls and teeth of the two main groups of plant-eaters. In the Jurassic Period sauropods such as *Diplodocus*, with their simple raking or chopping teeth and fermentation

digestion, were the most abundant plant-eaters. Their decline at the end of the Jurassic is mirrored, in the early Cretaceous, by an increase in the abundance of ornithopods like *Iguanodon*, which had grinding teeth and processed the food in their mouths. Flowering plants also made their appearance at this time. Is it possible that the grinders were better able to cope with the new kinds of plant food? This seems distinctly possible, especially as the most efficient grinders of all, hadrosaurs like *Edmontosaurus*, became the biggest and most successful group of

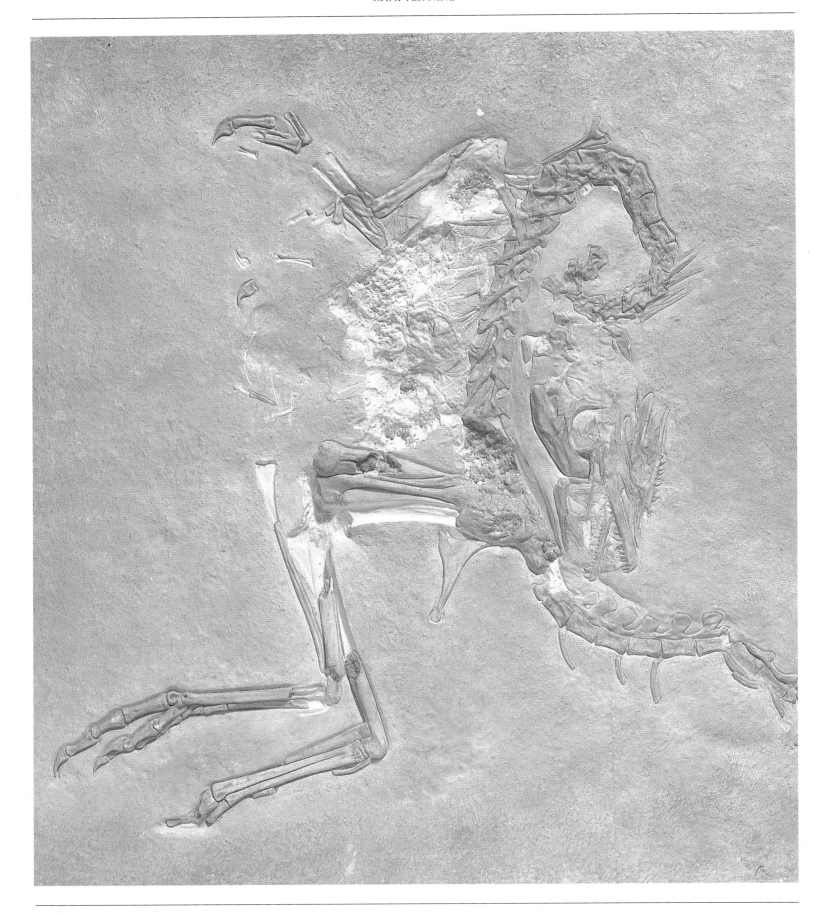

NAME	MEANING
Tyrannosaurus rex	King tyrant lizard
Diplodocus carnegiei	Carnegie's double beam
Deinonychus antirrhopus	Counterbalancing terrible claw
Iguanodon atherfieldensis	Iguana tooth from Atherfield
Iguanodon bernissartensis	Iguana tooth from Bernissart

DINOSAUR NAMES. Dinosaur names have two parts, both derived from Greek or Latin, as do all animals and plants. The first name identifies the genus and the second the species. In many cases there is only one dinosaur species in each genus, so just the first name is used as a "shorthand" version. When paleontologists choose the name of a new dinosaur they try to make it say something significant about the nature of the animal, where it was found, or who made the discovery.

very difficult to answer indeed, especially if there are vital bones missing from the specimen. But it is only on this basis that the dinosaur can be accurately classified.

The paleontologist is finally sure which main group the dinosaur belongs to. Now the skeleton must be minutely checked to see if it is one of a known species within that group or something that no one has described before. Again, this may be a very tricky task. After all, just when is a dinosaur different enough to count as "unknown" rather than just a variation of "known?" Sometimes even named specimens are re-examined and identified as being something else. There have been heated debates and even lifelong disputes between paleontologists on this subject.

Naming and publication of the dinosaur's description are the last duties of the paleontologist. This is a very formal process in which the bone by bone description must follow a strict formula with carefully reasoned deductions about the dinosaur itself. A panel of other experts reads and approves the paper before it is published in a scientific journal. The existence of

LAST MEAL. *Opposite:* Close examination of this saurischian *Compsognathus* revealed tiny bones of the lizard *Bavarisaurus* inside its ribs, presumably its last meal.

NATURE VOL. 324 27 NOVEMBER 1986

Baryonyx, a remarkable new theropod dinosaur

Alan J. Charig & Angela C. Milner

Department of Palaeontology, British Museum (Natural History), Cromwell Road, London SW7 5BD, UK

An extremely large claw bone, some 30 cm long, was found in Wealden (Lower Cretaceous) deposits in a Surrey claypit in January 1983. This led to the discovery the following month of the well-preserved skeleton of a new large theropod dinosaur. Only one other theropod specimen comprising more than a few bones had ever been found in Britain, and that discovery was more than a century ago. Indeed, no large theropod, reasonably complete, had previously been discovered in Lower Cretaceous rocks anywhere in the world. Our study so far suggests that the Surrey dinosaur was a typical large theropod in certain respects, resembling, for example *Allosaurus*[1]. In several other respects, however, it differs sufficiently from all known dinosaurs to merit designation as the representative of a new species, genus and family.

Family **Baryonychidae** nov.
Diagnosis. As for genus *Baryonyx*, below.
Genus *Baryonyx* nov.
Derivation of name. Gk, βᾰρύ, heavy, strong; "ονυξ, talon, claw.
Type-species. *B. walkeri* nov.
Diagnosis. As for species *B. walkeri*, below.
Species *Baryonyx walkeri* nov.
Derivation of name. For Mr William J. Walker, who found the first indication of the skeleton, namely the large claw bone (ungual phalanx).
Holotype. B.M.(N.H.) Palaeo. Dept. R. 9951.

THE *BARYONYX* STORY: IDENTIFICATION. After detailed study, The Natural History Museum paleontologists decided that the dinosaur was one of a new and unknown species. Its existence was officially announced in November 1986, nearly four years after the original discovery. It was named *Baryonyx walkeri*. *Baryonyx* from the Greek meaning "heavy claw," and *walkeri* in honor of the man who found the claw bone.

the new dinosaur is recognized from the exact date of publication. This may seem to involve a great deal of extra work but it is the paleontologist's most important task because it allows the new discovery to be understood by other scientists. With such a very small number of dinosaur skeletons to study (less than a dozen specimens of *Tyrannosaurus* have been discovered in the last 150 years,

for example, and only two or three reasonably complete skeletons), it is vital that paleontologists should know about what has been found in other parts of the world.

BRINGING DINOSAURS TO LIFE
Modeling the dinosaur and putting the skeleton on public display require yet more skills. Most full skeletons that you see in museums are actually replicas of originals. Fossil bones can indeed be mounted on heavy metal frames called armatures, but their weight and fragility make them difficult to display safely. Replicas, which can be made of light, hollow materials, such as glass fiber, and which weigh a fraction of the original, can be held in place with much thinner metal rods or plastic tubes, often running invisibly through the inside of the bones. The paleontologist will work with a team of technicians to ensure that the dinosaur is displayed safely, securely, and in the right stance.

Dinosaur modeling is a skill fully understood by only a few dozen people worldwide. The modeler must start with the paleontologist's bone and muscle reconstructions to get the basic body

CLADOGRAM. *Overleaf:* This shows some of the features that are used to identify different dinosaurs. By answering a series of "Does it have?" questions, you can work out the group it belongs to.

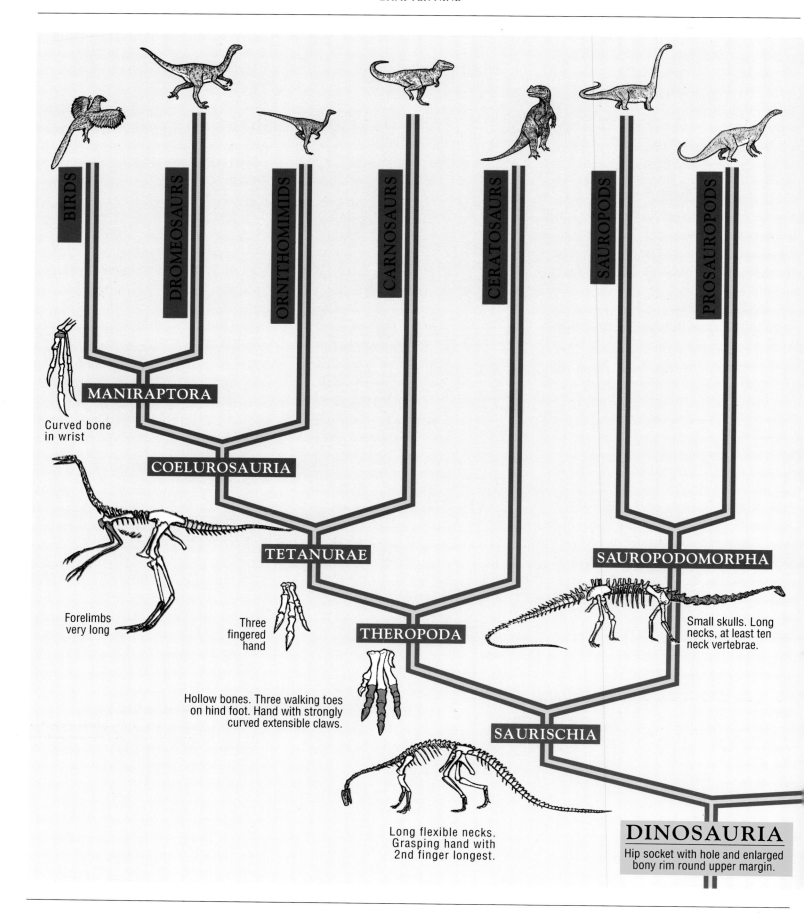

BIRDS

DROMEOSAURS

ORNITHOMIMIDS

CARNOSAURS

CERATOSAURS

SAUROPODS

PROSAUROPODS

MANIRAPTORA

Curved bone
in wrist

COELUROSAURIA

Forelimbs
very long

Three
fingered
hand

TETANURAE

SAUROPODOMORPHA

Small skulls. Long
necks, at least ten
neck vertebrae.

THEROPODA

Hollow bones. Three walking toes
on hind foot. Hand with strongly
curved extensible claws.

SAURISCHIA

Long flexible necks.
Grasping hand with
2nd finger longest.

DINOSAURIA
Hip socket with hole and enlarged
bony rim round upper margin.

LESOTHOSAURUS

STEGOSAURS

ANKYLOSAURS

HETERODONTOSAURS

HYPSILOPHODONTS

IGUANODONTS

HADROSAURS

PACHYCEPHALOSAURS

CERATOPIANS

EUORNITHOPODA

MARGINOCEPHALIA

THYREOPHORA

Jaw hinge below
level of tooth row

CERAPODA

Bony shelf at
back of skull

Bony plates (scutes)
embedded in rows
along back

GENASAURIA

Cheek teeth with
thickened enamel
on one side.

ORNITHISCHIA

Tooth row set
in from jaw margin
to form cheeks

Bird–hipped pelvis. Predentary
bone in lower jaw.

THE *BARYONYX* STORY: RECONSTRUCTION. The reconstructed skeleton of *Baryonyx* mounted in a lifelike running position.

shape of the dinosaur. Details such as teeth and claws are again based on the original description. Fossil claws, for example, are in fact only the bone core of the claw itself and need to be modeled up to a third larger. Skin texture added to the model is often based closely on the appearance of modern reptiles such as crocodiles as there is rarely any fossil skin to guide the model maker. Other details are not so clear cut. What color should the skin be? Mouth open or closed? Should the eyes have round

pupils like a bird or slit ones like a snake? There are no right answers to these questions, so the paleontologist and model maker must decide between them. If the dinosaur model or picture is to have a scenic setting, then the correct vegetation and landscape must also be created.

Despite the time it takes to prepare public displays of dinosaurs, most paleontologists love this part of their

work. For it is here that the discomfort of excavation, the years of painstaking preparation, the hours of research, cross-checking, and writing all come together. Suddenly we see some towering, jagged-toothed monster or plodding plant-eater as big as a house, some fleet-footed pack hunter, or ingenious scavenger. Like the wizard who conjures dragons out of a circle, the paleontologist can bring these astounding creatures to life, stepping toward us over millions of years of history.

RESTORING A DINOSAUR. *Opposite left:* The complete skeleton is reconstructed first. *Below:* Muscles are added to give the body shape and outline. *Above right:* The skin is added to create an authentic idea of what the dinosaur looked like, although we can only guess at the color.

John Holmes ~ 92

DINOSAUR DATA

T his alphabetical listing provides comparative information on the dinosaurs and other animals mentioned in this book. As well as providing a guide to the pronunciation and meaning of the name, there are details of the group to which each belongs, age, geological period, and size. Ages are given as accurately as possible. Where a range is given (e.g. 155–145 million years), it means that the animal lived within that time span, not for all of it. The illustrations shown are not to scale.

incertae sedis (group uncertain)

apatosaurus

Apatosaurus
Ah-pat-oh-sore-us • DECEPTIVE LIZARD

GROUP	Saurischia, Sauropoda
AGE	154–145 million years
PERIOD	Upper Jurassic
LOCALITY	USA
LENGTH	up to 70 feet

Albertosaurus
Al-burt-oh-sore-us • ALBERTA LIZARD

GROUP	Saurischia, Carnosauria
AGE	76–74 million years
PERIOD	Upper Cretaceous
LOCALITY	Canada
LENGTH	up to 30 feet

Allosaurus
Al-oh-sore-us • OTHER LIZARD

GROUP	Saurischia, Carnosauria
AGE	150–135 million years
PERIOD	Upper Jurassic
LOCALITY	USA
LENGTH	up to 50 feet

Anchisaurus
Ank-ee-sore-us • NEAR LIZARD

GROUP	Saurischia, Prosauropoda
AGE	200–190 million years
PERIOD	Upper Triassic
LOCALITY	USA
LENGTH	up to 6.5 feet

Archaeopteryx (not a dinosaur)
Ark-ee-opt-erics • ANCIENT WING

GROUP	Saurischia, Aviales
AGE	147 million years
PERIOD	Upper Jurassic
LOCALITY	Germany
LENGTH	up to 18 inches

Avimimus
Aa-vee-meem-us • BIRD MIMIC

GROUP	Saurischia, Theropoda*
AGE	about 75 million years
PERIOD	Upper Cretaceous
LOCALITY	Mongolia
LENGTH	up to 5 feet

Barosaurus
Bar-oh-sore-us • HEAVY LIZARD

GROUP	Saurischia, Sauropoda
AGE	155–145 million years
PERIOD	Upper Jurassic
LOCALITY	USA
LENGTH	up to 80 feet

Baryonyx
Bar-ee-on-icks • HEAVY CLAW

GROUP	Saurischia, Theropoda*
AGE	about 124 million years
PERIOD	Lower Cretaceous
LOCALITY	England
LENGTH	34 feet

Brachiosaurus
Brak-ee-oh-sore-us • ARM LIZARD

GROUP	Saurischia, Sauropoda
AGE	155–140 million years
PERIOD	Upper Jurassic
LOCALITY	Tanzania, USA
LENGTH	up to 75 feet

camarasaurus

Camarasaurus
Kam-ahra-sore-us • CHAMBERED LIZARD

GROUP	Saurischia, Sauropoda
AGE	155–145 million years
PERIOD	Upper Jurassic
LOCALITY	USA
LENGTH	up to 65 feet

Camptosaurus

Kamp-toe-sore-us • BENT LIZARD

GROUP	Ornithischia, Ornithopoda
AGE	155–145 million years
PERIOD	Upper Jurassic
LOCALITY	USA
LENGTH	up to 16 feet

centrosaurus

Centrosaurus

Sent-row-sore-us • HORNED LIZARD

GROUP	Ornithischia, Ceratopia
AGE	76–74 million years
PERIOD	Upper Cretaceous
LOCALITY	Canada
LENGTH	up to 16 feet

Chasmosaurus

Kas-mow-sore-us • CLEFT LIZARD

GROUP	Ornithischia, Ceratopia
AGE	76–74 million years
PERIOD	Upper Cretaceous
LOCALITY	Canada
LENGTH	up to 16 feet

Coelophysis

Seel-oh-fie-sis • HOLLOW FORM

GROUP	Saurischia, Coelurosauria
AGE	225–220 million years
PERIOD	Upper Triassic
LOCALITY	USA
LENGTH	up to 10 feet

Coelurus

Seel-ure-us • HOLLOW TAIL

GROUP	Saurischia, Coelurosauria
AGE	155–145 million years
PERIOD	Upper Jurassic
LOCALITY	USA
LENGTH	up to 8 feet

Compsognathus

Komp-sog-nay-thus • PRETTY JAW

GROUP	Saurischia, Coelurosauria
AGE	147 million years
PERIOD	Upper Jurassic
LOCALITY	Germany
LENGTH	26 inches

Corythosaurus

Cor-ith-oh-sore-us • HELMET LIZARD

GROUP	Ornithischia, Ornithopoda
AGE	76–74 million years
PERIOD	Upper Cretaceous
LOCALITY	Canada, USA
LENGTH	up to 33 feet

Craspedodon

Krass-pede-oh-don • EDGE TOOTH

GROUP	Ornithischia, Ornithopoda
AGE	86–83 million years
PERIOD	Upper Cretaceous
LOCALITY	Belgium
LENGTH	unknown

Dacentrurus

Dah-sent-rue-rus • POINTED TAIL

GROUP	Ornithischia, Stegosauria
AGE	157–152 million years
PERIOD	Upper Jurassic
LOCALITY	France, England, Portugal
LENGTH	perhaps about 20 feet

Deinocheirus

Dine-oh-kire-us • TERRIBLE HAND

GROUP	Saurischia, Ornithomimosauria
AGE	70–65 million years
PERIOD	Upper Cretaceous
LOCALITY	Mongolia
LENGTH	unknown, arms are 10 feet long

Deinonychus

Die-non-i-kus • TERRIBLE CLAW

GROUP	Saurischia, Dromaeosauria
AGE	110 million years
PERIOD	Lower Cretaceous
LOCALITY	USA
LENGTH	up to 11 feet

Diplodocus

Di-ploh-dok-us • DOUBLE BEAM

GROUP	Saurischia, Sauropoda
AGE	155–145 million years
PERIOD	Upper Cretaceous
LOCALITY	USA
LENGTH	up to 90 feet

Dromaeosaurus

Dro-may-oh-sore-us • RUNNING LIZARD

GROUP	Saurischia, Dromaeosauroidea
AGE	76–74 million years
PERIOD	Upper Cretaceous
LOCALITY	Canada
LENGTH	up to 6 feet

Dryosaurus

Dry-oh-sore-us • OAK LIZARD

GROUP	Ornithischia, Ornithopoda
AGE	155–140 million years
PERIOD	Upper Jurassic
LOCALITY	Tanzania, USA
LENGTH	up to 13 feet

edmontosaurus

Dryptosaurus
Drip-toe-sore-us • WOUNDING LIZARD

GROUP	Saurischia, Carnosauria
AGE	74–65 million years
PERIOD	Upper Cretaceous
LOCALITY	USA
LENGTH	perhaps about 16 feet

Edmontonia
Ed-mont-own-ee-ah • OF EDMONTON

GROUP	Ornithischia, Ankylosauria
AGE	76–74 million years
PERIOD	Upper Cretaceous
LOCALITY	Canada
LENGTH	about 13 feet

Edmontosaurus
Ed-mont-oh-sore-us • EDMONTON LIZARD

GROUP	Ornithischia, Ornithopoda
AGE	76–65 million years
PERIOD	Upper Cretaceous
LOCALITY	Canada
LENGTH	up to 43 feet

Elasmosaurus (not a dinosaur)
Ee-laz-mow-sore-us • RIBBON LIZARD

GROUP	Plesiosauria
AGE	70–65 million years
PERIOD	Upper Cretaceous
LOCALITY	USA
LENGTH	up to 40 feet

Euoplocephalus
You-op-loh-keff-ah-lus • WELL-ARMOURED HEAD

GROUP	Ornithischia, Ankylosauria
AGE	about 71 million years
PERIOD	Upper Cretaceous
LOCALITY	Canada
LENGTH	up to 20 feet

euoplocephalus

Euparkeria (not a dinosaur)
You-park-ear-ee-ah • OF PARKER'S

GROUP	Archosauria
AGE	245–241 million years
PERIOD	Lower Triassic
LOCALITY	South Africa
LENGTH	about 3 feet

Gallimimus
Gal-lee-meem-us • CHICKEN MIMIC

GROUP	Saurischia, Ornithomimosauria
AGE	74–70 million years
PERIOD	Upper Cretaceous
LOCALITY	Mongolia
LENGTH	up to 18 feet

Gilmoreosaurus
Gil-more-oh-sore-us • GILMORE'S LIZARD

GROUP	Ornithischia, Ornithopoda
AGE	80–70 million years
PERIOD	Upper Cretaceous
LOCALITY	China
LENGTH	perhaps about 20 feet

Hadrosaurus
Had-row-sore-us • BIG LIZARD

GROUP	Ornithischia, Ornithopoda
AGE	83–74 million years
PERIOD	Upper Cretaceous
LOCALITY	USA
LENGTH	up to 26 feet

Herrerasaurus
Herr-air-ah-sore-us • HERRERA LIZARD

GROUP	Dinosauria
AGE	230–225 million years
PERIOD	Upper Triassic
LOCALITY	Argentina
LENGTH	up to 10 feet

hypsilophodon

iguanodon

Hylaeosaurus
High-lay-ee-oh-sore-us • WOODLAND LIZARD

GROUP	Ornithischia, Ankylosauria
AGE	150–135 million years
PERIOD	Lower Cretaceous
LOCALITY	England
LENGTH	up to 13 feet

Hypsilophodon
Hip-sih-loh-foe-don • HIGH RIDGE TOOTH

GROUP	Ornithischia, Ornithopoda
AGE	about 125 million years
PERIOD	Lower Cretaceous
LOCALITY	England
LENGTH	up to 7.5 feet

Iguanodon
Ig-wha-noh-don • IGUANA TOOTH

GROUP	Ornithischia, Ornithopoda
AGE	130–115 million years
PERIOD	Lower Cretaceous
LOCALITY	Belg., Eng., Ger., Spain, USA
LENGTH	up to 33 feet

Kentrosaurus
Kent-row-sore-us • SPIKY LIZARD

GROUP	Ornithischia, Stegosauria
AGE	about 140 million years
PERIOD	Upper Jurassic
LOCALITY	Tanzania
LENGTH	up to 10 feet

Kritosaurus

Krit-oh-sore-us • NOBLE LIZARD

GROUP	Ornithischia, Ornithopoda
AGE	80–75 million years
PERIOD	Upper Cretaceous

LOCALITY	USA
LENGTH	up to 26 feet

Lagosuchus (not a dinosaur)

Lag-oh-sue-kus • RABBIT CROCODILE

GROUP	Dinosauromorpha
AGE	241–235 million years
PERIOD	Middle Triassic
LOCALITY	Argentina
LENGTH	about 12 inches

Lambeosaurus

Lam-bee-oh-sore-us • LAMBE'S LIZARD

GROUP	Ornithischia, Ornithopoda
AGE	76–74 million years
PERIOD	Upper Cretaceous
LOCALITY	Canada
LENGTH	up to 30 feet

Maiasaura

My-ah-sore-ah • GOOD MOTHER LIZARD

GROUP	Ornithischia, Ornithopoda
AGE	80–75 million years
PERIOD	Upper Cretaceous
LOCALITY	USA
LENGTH	up to 30 feet

Mamenchisaurus

Mah-men-chi-sore-us • MAMENCHI LIZARD

GROUP	Saurischia, Sauropoda
AGE	155–145 million years
PERIOD	Upper Jurassic
LOCALITY	China
LENGTH	up to 72 feet

Massospondylus

Mass-oh-spon-di-lus • MASSIVE VERTEBRA

GROUP	Saurischia, Prosauropoda
AGE	208–204 million years
PERIOD	Lower Jurassic
LOCALITY	South Africa
LENGTH	up to 13 feet

Megalosaurus

Meg-ah-low-sore-us • BIG LIZARD

GROUP	Saurischia, Carnosauria
AGE	170–155 million years
PERIOD	Jurassic
LOCALITY	England, Tanzania
LENGTH	up to 30 feet

Ornitholestes

Orn-ith-oh-lest-eez • BIRD ROBBER

GROUP	Saurischia, Coelurosauria
AGE	155–145 million years
PERIOD	Upper Jurassic
LOCALITY	USA
LENGTH	up to 6.5 feet

ouranosaurus

Ornithopsis

Orn-ith-op-sis • BIRD-LIKE STRUCTURE

GROUP	Saurischia, Sauropoda
AGE	about 125 million years
PERIOD	Lower Cretaceous
LOCALITY	England
LENGTH	unknown, perhaps 65 feet

Orodromeus

Ore-oh-drom-ee-us • MOUNTAIN RUNNER

GROUP	Ornithischia, Ornithopoda
AGE	about 74 million years
PERIOD	Upper Cretaceous
LOCALITY	USA
LENGTH	up to 6.5 feet

Ouranosaurus

Oo-ran-oh-sore-us • BRAVE MONITOR LIZARD

GROUP	Ornithischia, Ornithopoda
AGE	about 115 million years
PERIOD	Lower Cretaceous
LOCALITY	Niger
LENGTH	up to 23 feet

Oviraptor

Oh-vee-rap-tor • EGG THIEF

GROUP	Saurischia, Oviraptorosauria
AGE	85–75 million years
PERIOD	Upper Cretaceous
LOCALITY	Mongolia
LENGTH	up to 6 feet

Pachycephalosaurus

Pack-ee-keff-ah-low-sore-us • THICK-HEADED LIZARD

GROUP	Ornithischia, Pachycephalosauria
AGE	about 67 million years

parasaurolophus

PERIOD	Upper Cretaceous
LOCALITY	USA
LENGTH	up to 26 feet

scelidosaurus

Pachyrhinosaurus
Pack-ee-rine-oh-sore-us • THICK-NOSED LIZARD

GROUP	Ornithischia, Ceratopia
AGE	76–74 million years
PERIOD	Upper Cretaceous
LOCALITY	Canada, USA
LENGTH	up to 20 feet

Parasaurolophus
Par-ah-sore-ol-oh-fus • LIKE SAUROLOPHUS

GROUP	Ornithischia, Ornithopoda
AGE	76–74 million years
PERIOD	Upper Cretaceous
LOCALITY	Canada, USA
LENGTH	up to 33 feet

Parksosaurus
Parks-oh-sore-us • PARKS' LIZARD

GROUP	Ornithischia, Ornithopoda
AGE	76–74 million years
PERIOD	Upper Cretaceous
LOCALITY	Canada
LENGTH	up to 10 feet

Pelorosaurus
Pel-oh-row-sore-us • MONSTROUS LIZARD

GROUP	Saurischia, Sauropoda
AGE	about 150 million years
PERIOD	Upper Jurassic
LOCALITY	England
LENGTH	unknown, perhaps 65–80 feet

Plateosaurus
Plat-ee-oh-sore-us • FLAT LIZARD

GROUP	Saurischia, Prosauropoda
AGE	about 210 million years
PERIOD	Upper Triassic
LOCALITY	France, Germany, Switzerland
LENGTH	up to 23 feet

Protoceratops
Pro-toe-ker-ah-tops • FIRST HORNED FACE

GROUP	Ornithischia, Ceratopia
AGE	85–80 million years
PERIOD	Upper Cretaceous
LOCALITY	Mongolia
LENGTH	up to 6 feet

Psittacosaurus
Sit-ak-oh-sore-us • PARROT LIZARD

GROUP	Ornithischia, Ceratopia
AGE	124–97 million years
PERIOD	Upper Cretaceous
LOCALITY	China, Mongolia, Russia
LENGTH	up to 6 feet

Quetzalcoatlus (not a dinosaur)
Kwet-zal-co-art-lus • FOR QUETZALCOATL

GROUP	Pterosauria
AGE	67–65 million years
PERIOD	Upper Cretaceous
LOCALITY	USA
LENGTH	wing span up to 36 feet

Rhabdodon
Rab-doe-don • ROD TOOTH

GROUP	Ornithischia, Ornithopoda
AGE	83–70 million years
PERIOD	Upper Cretaceous
LOCALITY	Austria, France, Spain, Romania
LENGTH	up to 10 feet

Saurolophus
Sore-ol-oh-fus • RIDGED LIZARD

GROUP	Ornithischia, Ornithopoda
AGE	74–70 million years
PERIOD	Upper Cretaceous
LOCALITY	Canada, Mongolia
LENGTH	up to 40 feet

psittacosaurus

Saurornithoides
Sore-orn-ith-oy-deez • BIRD-LIKE LIZARD

GROUP	Saurischia, Dromaeosauroidea
AGE	80–74 million years
PERIOD	Upper Cretaceous
LOCALITY	Canada
LENGTH	up to 6.5 feet

Scartopus
Skar-toe-pus • NIMBLE FOOT

GROUP	Saurischia, Coelurosauria
AGE	about 95 million years
PERIOD	Upper Cretaceous
LOCALITY	Australia
LENGTH	unknown

stegosaurus

Scelidosaurus
Skel-ide-oh-sore-us • LIMB LIZARD

GROUP	Ornithischia, Thyreophora
AGE	203–194 million years
PERIOD	Lower Jurassic
LOCALITY	England
LENGTH	up to 13 feet

Segnosaurus

Seg-no-sore-us • SLOW LIZARD

GROUP	Saurischia*
AGE	97–88 million years
PERIOD	Upper Cretaceous
LOCALITY	Mongolia
LENGTH	up to 13 feet

STYRACOSAURUS

tyrannosaurus

Stegosaurus

Steg-oh-sore-us • ROOF LIZARD

GROUP	Ornithischia, Stegosauria
AGE	155–145 million years
PERIOD	Upper Jurassic
LOCALITY	USA
LENGTH	up to 30 feet

Struthiosaurus

Strew-thee-oh-sore-us • OSTRICH LIZARD

GROUP	Ornithischia, Ankylosauria
AGE	83–75 million years
PERIOD	Upper Cretaceous
LOCALITY	Austria, Romania
LENGTH	up to 6.5 feet

Styracosaurus

Sty-rack-oh-sore-us • SPIKED LIZARD

GROUP	Ornithischia, Ceratopia
AGE	85–80 million years
PERIOD	Upper Cretaceous
LOCALITY	Canada, USA
LENGTH	up to 18 feet

Tenontosaurus

Ten-on-toe-sore-us • SINEW LIZARD

GROUP	Ornithischia, Ornithopoda
AGE	110 million years
PERIOD	Lower Cretaceous
LOCALITY	USA
LENGTH	up to 21 feet

Triceratops

Try-ker-ah-tops • THREE-HORNED FACE

GROUP	Ornithischia, Ceratopia
AGE	67–65 million years
PERIOD	Upper Cretaceous
LOCALITY	USA
LENGTH	up to 30 feet

Troodon

True-oh-don • WOUNDING TOOTH

GROUP	Saurischia, Dromaeosauroidea
AGE	75–70 million years
PERIOD	Upper Cretaceous
LOCALITY	Canada, USA
LENGTH	up to 8 feet

Tuojiangosaurus

Two-yang-oh-sore-us • TUOJIANG LIZARD

GROUP	Ornithischia, Stegosauria
AGE	157–154 million years
PERIOD	Upper Jurassic
LOCALITY	China
LENGTH	up to 21 feet

Tyrannosaurus

Tie-ran-oh-sore-us • TYRANT LIZARD

GROUP	Saurischia, Carnosauria
AGE	67– 65 million years
PERIOD	Upper Cretaceous
LOCALITY	USA
LENGTH	up to 40 feet

Velociraptor

Vel-oss-ee-rap-tor • QUICK PLUNDERER

GROUP	Saurischia, Dromaeosauroidea
AGE	84–80 million years
PERIOD	Upper Cretaceous
LOCALITY	China, Mongolia
LENGTH	up to 6 feet

GLOSSARY

anatomy — the structure of an animal.

angiosperms — flowering plants.

ankylosaurs — armored ornithischian dinosaurs.

archosaurs — a major group of reptiles that includes the living crocodiles, and dinosaurs, pterosaurs, and thecodontians which are all extinct.

bipedal — walking on two legs.

carnivore — meat-eater.

carnosaurs — large, heavily-built theropod dinosaurs.

ceratopians — four-legged ornithischian dinosaurs with horns and neck frills.

coelurosaurs — small to medium-sized slenderly built theropod dinosaurs.

conifers — cone-bearing trees such as pines and firs.

Cretaceous — the third and last Period in the Mesozoic Era, from 145 to 65 million years ago.

cycads — short-trunked plants with rather palmlike leaves that were common in the Mesozoic Era.

dinosaurs — land-dwelling reptiles with upright stance that lived between 230 and 65 million years ago.

evolution — gradual change in the characteristics of animals and plants brought about by natural selection acting on successive generations.

extinction — dying out of a species.

fossil — remains of once living organisms that are preserved usually by burial and chemical change.

gastroliths — stomach stones used for grinding up food.

Gondwana — southern hemisphere super-continent that existed in Triassic times incorporating Africa, Antarctica, Australia, India, Madagascar, and South America.

hadrosaurs — duck-billed ornithopod dinosaurs with multiple rows of grinding teeth.

herbivore — plant-eater.

ichthyosaurs — marine reptiles with a streamlined, superficially dolphinlike appearance that lived in the seas during the Mesozoic Era.

Jurassic — the middle Period in the Mesozoic Era, from 213 to 145 million years ago.

Laurasia — northern hemisphere supercontinent which existed in Triassic times incorporating Asia, Europe, and North America.

ligaments — bundles of tough fibrous tissue that link together the bones of a skeleton and support the joints.

mammals — backboned animals that have hair and feed their young on milk.

mammal-like reptiles — group of reptiles that lived mainly in Triassic and earlier times from which mammals evolved.

Mesozoic — "Middle life," the major time span (era) 245–65 million years ago, informally known as "the age of dinosaurs."

ornithischians — dinosaurs with a hip structure in which the two lower bones on each side lie parallel and point backward; all ornithischians were plant-eaters.

ornithopods — primarily bipedal ornithischian dinosaurs that developed specialized teeth to grind up tough vegetation.

pachycephalosaurs — bipedal ornithischian dinosaurs with thickened "dome-headed" skulls.

paleontologist — a person who studies fossils.

Pangaea — the single land mass formed by the collision of all the continents. This happened long before the earliest dinosaurs appeared by which time Pangaea had begun to separate into Laurasia and Gondwana.

plesiosaurs — fish-eating marine reptiles with four flippers that lived in the Mesozoic Era.

prosauropods — one of the earliest groups of dinosaurs, these long-necked saurischian plant-eaters with large thumb claws were distributed world-wide and died out in the early Jurassic.

pterosaurs — flying reptiles that lived during the Mesozoic Era; they were close relatives of the dinosaurs.

quadrupedal — walking on four legs.

reptile — backboned animal that is "cold-blooded," has a scaly skin and lays eggs.

saurischians — dinosaurs with a hip structure in which the two lower bones on each side point in opposite directions.

sauropods — large quadrupedal saurischian plant-eating dinosaurs, with very long necks and tails.

scavenger — meat-eater that feeds on dead animals, sometimes by stealing kills from a hunter.

spine — backbone (see under vertebra).

stegosaurs — plant-eating dinosaurs with tall plates running along their backs and two pairs of tail spikes.

tendon — tough inelastic tissue that joins muscles to bones.

thecodontians — early archosaurs from which crocodiles, dinosaurs, and pterosaurs evolved during the Triassic Period.

theropods — a group of saurischian dinosaurs that includes all the meat-eaters; almost all were bipedal.

trackway — a series of footprints left as an animal walks over soft ground.

Triassic — the first Period in the Mesozoic Era, from 248 to 213 million years ago.

vertebra — a single bone from the back. A chain of vertebrae makes up the backbone.

FURTHER READING

Books about Dinosaurs

Charig, A. J.
A New Look at the Dinosaurs.
New York, Facts on File, 1979.
(Reprinted with amendments 1983.)

Czerkas, S. J. and Olson, E. C.
Dinosaurs Past and Present. Volumes I and II.
Seattle, University of Washington Press, 1987.

Dodson, P. (Ed.)
Encyclopedia of Dinosaurs.
Lincolnwood, Illinois, Publications International Ltd., 1990.

Lambert, D.
Dinosaur Data Book.
New York, Avon, 1990.

Lindsay, W.
The Great Dinosaur Atlas.
New York, Julian Messner, 1991.

Milner, A. C.
The Dinosaur Wall Chart.
London, Studio Editions, 1991.

Norman, D. B.
The Illustrated Encyclopedia of Dinosaurs.
New York, Crescent, 1985.

Norman, D. B.
Dinosaurs!
New York, Prentice Hall, 1991.

Norman, D. B. and Milner A. C.
Dinosaur. Eyewitness Guides 13.
New York, Alfred A. Knopf, 1989.

Books about other Fossils

Benton, M. J.
The Reign of the Reptiles.
New Jersey, Outlet, 1990.

Taylor, P. D.
Fossil. Eyewitness Guides 19.
New York, Alfred A. Knopf, 1990.

Wellnhofer, P.
The Illustrated Encyclopedia of Pterosaurs.
New York, Crescent, 1991.

Collecting and Preparing Fossils

Croucher, R. and Woolley, A. R.
Fossils, Minerals and Rocks. Collection and Preservation.
London, British Museum (Natural History) / Cambridge University Press, 1982.

INDEX

A
adaptability *see* evolution
adventure stories, dinosaurs in 103
Africa, East in Jurassic Period **16**
Albertosaurus 19, 28, **30**, 61, 70, 99
alligators 75, 86-7
Allosaurus 17, **34**, 39, 41-2, **41**, 110-11
Alvarez, Luis *and* Walter 83
America, North **16**, 19, 25, 35, 58-9, **68**, 80, 90, 99
    prime area of study 82, **82**
    see also USA
American Museum of Natural History 101
ammonites 81
amphibians 81
anacondas **52**
anatomy, comparative, as source of information 12-13, 34, 110
Anchisaurus 90
Andrews, Roy Chapman 101, **101**
angiosperms *see* flowering plants
ankle joints 12, **14**, 22
ankylosaurs 38, **39**, 73
Antarctica, finds in 102
antelopes 38, 56, 59
ants 57
Apatosaurus 17, **22**, 39, **69**, 72, 109-10
Archaeopteryx 17, **19**
archosaurs 12, **14**, 17
Arctic finds 102
Argentina, finds in 13
armadillos **46**
armor 46-8, **46**, **47**, **48**, 71
arms 27-8, **51**
arthropods 12
asteroid theory of extinction 83-5, **83**, **84**, **85**, 87
attack 46-7, **46**, **49**, 50, 53
Australia, finds in 30-1, **31**
Avimimus 71

B
Barosaurus 35
Baryonyx walkeri 43, **76**, **106-111**, **113**, **116**
    see also Britain, finds in
Bavarisaurus 43, **113**
beaks 37, **38**
bears 57
bees 17
beetles 61, 80
belemnites 81
Belgium, finds in 97, **97**
bennettitaleans **16**, **17**
Berlin, Humboldt Museum in **100**
Bernissart (Belgium), find at 97, **97**
Bible and creation 90-1
bighorn sheep **46**

bird-hipped dinosaurs *see* ornithiscians
birds **13**, 17, 19, **19**, 29, 35, 72, 73, 74, 76, 81
blood 39, 41, 75-7
"bone beds" 58-9, **58**, 97
bone structures 68-9, **68**, **69**, **70**, **76**, 77
    bony plates **47**, 48, **50**, 71
brachiopods 81
Brachiosaurus **16**, 17, 23, 25, **25**, 47, 72, **100**
    blood 76
    diet 34
    muscles **70**
brains 72-3, **72**, **73**, 74, 75
Britain, finds in 90-5
    see also Baryonyx walkeri
Brontosaurus see Apatosaurus
Brookes, R. **90**
Brown, Barnum 99
Buckland, Dr William 92, 94, **94**, 95
buffaloes 38, **39**
    "giant buffalo" 90

C
Camarasaurus 109, 110
camouflage 50-3
Camptosaurus 39
Canadian finds 58-9, 99
cannibalism **42**, 43
cape buffalo **39**
caribou 80
Carnegie, Andrew **90**, **98**
carnosaurs *see* meat-eaters
cartilage 29
Centrosaurus **58**, 59, 99
ceratopians 30, 58, 73, 80
Chang Qu 90
Chasmosaurus **16**
cheeks 36, **37**
chewing 36-7, **37**
China, finds in 90, **91**, 101-2, **101**
cladograms **113**
clams 81
classification 111, 113, **113**
claws 22, **24**, 27-8, 42, 48, 50, **51**, 71, 116
climate 10, 14, 17, 19, 77
    and dinosaur extinction 80, 82, **82**, 85, 87
clubs, tail *see* tails
cooperative hunting 57-8, 74
Coelophysis **14**, **42**, 43
coelurosaurs 17, 73
Coelurus 17
cold-blooded? 39, 41, 75-7
color 11, **50**, 53, 71
    vision 73
comic strip dinosaurs 103
competition determining social order 48, 50
Compsognathus 42, 43, 97, **113**

condors 39
conifers **16**, 17, 36, 81
Cope, Edward Drinker 98-9, **98**
Corythosaurus 53, **68**, 99
Craspedodon 19
creation theories 90
    "creationists" 103
crested hadrosaurs 53, 59, **59**, 60
Cretaceous Period **16**, **17**, 19, **68**, 80, 99
    K–T boundary 82-3, **83**, 84, 85, **85**, 86
crocodiles **13**, 16, **16**, 22, 61, 86
Cuvier, Baron Georges 92, 94
cycads **16**, 17, 37

D
Dacentrurus 97
Deccan Traps volcanic area 85-6, **86**, 87
deer **81**
defense 46-50, 59, 71
Deinonychus **10**, **16**, 42, 50, **51**, 58, 74, 77
    antirrhopus **113**
diet 32-43, 108
dinosaur, origin of the name 94
Diplodocus 17, 22-3, **24**, 25, **25**, 34-5, **34**, 77, 111
    carnegiei **90**, **98**, 113
    hunted 39, 41-2, 47, 48
    legs 69-70
disease **74**
dodo **81**
Dollo, Louis 97, **97**, 99
dragons 91
Dromeosaurus 19, 42
Dryosaurus 48, 68, **69**, 101
Dryptosaurus (*Laelaps*) 97
ducks 35

E
ears 73-4, **73**
Edmontosaurus 30, 36-7, **37**, **50**, 53, **57**, 80, **80**, 111
Edwards, Vernon **102**
eggs 11, **11**, 38, **40**, 56, 59-61, **61**, 64
    and extinction theories 86-7
Elasmosaurus 99
elephants 34, 56, 64, 72, 75
environment and evolution 10, 80
Euoplocephalus 38, 46-7, **47**, 48
Euparkeria **23**
Europe in Triassic Period **16**
evolution
    of dinosaurs 12-19
        general theory 10, 80, 87
        opposing beliefs 103
extinction 80-7, **87**
eyes **46**, 50, **72**, 73, **73**, 116

Picture Acknowledgements Cover John Sibbick/NHM; pp. 8–9 John Sibbick/NHM; p. 10 Jenny Halstead–Imagination; p. 12 Andrew Milner; pp. 13–15 Ray Burrows; p. 16 (l) Sally Dray, (r) © 1991, Studio Editions reprinted from *The Dinosaur Wall Chart* by permission of the publisher; pp. 20–1 John Sibbick/NHM; p. 23 (l) Imagination; p. 24 (tl) G.B. Corbet/NHM, (mtl) Andrew Milner, (mbl) Gunter Ziesler/Bruce Coleman, (bl) Wayne Lankinen/Bruce Coleman, (b) Wayne Lankinen/Bruce Coleman; p. 25 Salamander Books Ltd., London; p. 26 (b) Imagination; p. 27 (tl) E. & P. Bauer/Bruce Coleman; p. 28 (tl) Jenny Halstead, (b) John Sibbick/NHM; p. 29 Neg. 315110, Courtesy Dept. Library Services, American Museum of Natural History; p. 30 (r) J. & D. Bartlett/Bruce Coleman; p. 31 (r) Imagination; pp. 32–3 John Sibbick/NHM; p. 37 (t) Jenny Halstead; p. 39 (tm) Peter Johnson/NHPA, (bm) William S. Paton/Bruce Coleman; p. 41 (tl) Jane Burton/Bruce Coleman; p. 46 (t) Gerald Cubitt/Bruce Coleman, (b) Pictor; p. 47 (t) John Sibbick/NHM; p. 48 (l) Salamander Books Ltd., London; p. 48 (r) and p. 49 John Sibbick/NHM; pp. 50–1 Peabody Museum, Yale University; p. 52 (l) Jenny Halstead, (tr) Austin James Stevens/Bruce Coleman, (mr) Bruce Davidson/Survival Anglia, (br) Rod Williams/Bruce Coleman; p. 53 Salamander Books Ltd., London; pp. 54–5 and p. 57 (t) John Sibbick/NHM; p. 57 (m) Rafi Ben-Shahar/OSF; p. 58 (t) John Sibbick/NHM, (m) Royal Tyrrell Museum/Alberta Culture and Multiculturalism; p. 59 and p. 60 (t) John Sibbick/NHM; p. 60 (b) Jenny Halstead; p. 65 (t) John Sibbick/NHM; pp. 66–7 John Sibbick/NHM; p. 69 (r) Ray Burrows; p. 70 (l) Jenny Halstead; p. 71 John Sibbick/NHM; p. 73 (b) and p. 75 (b) Jenny Halstead; p. 76 R.E.H. Reid; p.81 (bl) Eric Albert, (br) Michael Long/NHM; p. 82 © Douglas Henderson from *Dinosaurs – A Global View* by Sylvis and Stephen Czerkas, Dragon's World Ltd.; p. 83 (tl) Glen A. Izett/US Geological Survey, (tl) Harry Foster reproduced with the permission of the Canadian Museum of Nature, Ottawa, (b) © Royal Observatory, Edinburgh; p. 85 (t) US Geological Survey, (b) Ray Burrows; p. 86 (l) Hjalmar R. Bardarson/OSF, (r) K.G. Cox, Oxford University; p. 87 Bill Tidy; p.91 (l) The Dover Pictorial Archive Series, (r) From *Dinosaurs from China*, China Ocean Press; pp. 96–7 Dept. of Palaeontology, Royal Belgian Institute of Natural Sciences, Brussels; p. 100 (main pic.) Museum für Naturkunde, Tölke, Berlin; p. 101 (r) Neg. 410764, Courtesy Dept. Library Services, American Museum of Natural History, (ml and b) Mee–Mann Chang/Institute of Vertebrate Palaeontology and Palaeoanthropology, Beijing; p. 103 © 1992, Hanna–Barbera Productions, Inc. Licensed by C.P.L.; p. 106 Ray Burrows; p. 109 (b) and p. 111 John Holmes; p. 113 Reprinted with permission from *Nature* Vol. 324, 27 November 1986, Macmillan Magazines Ltd.; pp. 114–15 Ray Burrows; pp. 116–17 (b) John Holmes; pp. 118–24 Salamander Books Ltd., London. All other pictures are from The Natural History Museum, London. (*Key*: t = top; m = middle; l = left; r = right; b = bottom; NHM = The Natural History Museum, London.)